WHAT TO DO WHEN SOMEONE DIES

WHAT TO DO WHEN SOMEONE DIES

a Consumer Publication

Consumers' Association
publishers of **Which?**
14 Buckingham Street
London WC2N 6DS

a Consumer Publication

edited by   Edith Rudinger

published by   Consumers' Association
publishers of **Which?**

© Consumers' Association 1967
revised edition September 1986

ISBN 0 340 39963 5
and   0 85202 338 3

Photoset by Paston Press, Norwich
Printed and bound in Great Britain

The book deals mainly with the formalities and procedure in England and Wales; the important differences which apply in Scotland are given on pages 44–48 and on pages 103–104.

CONTENTS

Throughout this book

for 'he' read 'he or she'

FOREWORD

This book aims to help those who have never had to deal with the arrangements that must be made after a death – getting a doctor's certificate and registering the death, deciding whether to bury or cremate, choosing an undertaker and a coffin, putting notices in the papers, selecting the form of service, claiming national insurance benefits. It explains the function of people with whom they will come in contact, often for the first time. They will get help and guidance from the doctor, the registrar, the undertaker, the clergyman, the cemetery or crematorium officials, the Department of Health and Social Security and, in some circumstances, the police and the coroner. However, it is the executor or nearest relative who has to make the decisions, often at a time of personal distress. *What to do when someone dies* describes what needs to be done, when, and how to set about it.

No attempt is made to deal with the personal or social aspects of death and bereavement, such as the psychology of grief and shock, the rituals and conventions of mourning, or attitudes to death.

DEATH

You may discover someone apparently dead, and it can be difficult to tell whether he really is dead or not. For instance, someone rescued from water may appear not to breathe, yet might be revived by artificial respiration or 'kiss of life'.

The body temperature drops at the rate of one to two degrees centigrade an hour for the first few hours after death, so someone who has been dead for an hour or so is appreciably colder than normal. The extremities – feet and hands – get cold first. But very low body temperature alone is not a sure sign of death because comatose or unconscious people can also seem abnormally cold.

If there is any doubt whether someone is dead, treat him as being still alive.

telling the doctor
The first thing to do is to call the doctor. If you do not know how or where to get hold of a doctor, dial '999' for the emergency ambulance service.

Even if it seems certain that the person really is dead, you should let his doctor know soon. But if the doctor had been in attendance and the death was not unexpected, there may be no need to telephone him in the middle of the night instead of waiting until the next morning. Ask whether the doctor is going to come. If the death was peaceful and expected, the doctor may not feel it necessary to see the body, or may not come straightaway. Some doctors make it a practice to see the body of every patient who has died.

You should tell the doctor if the body is to be cremated because, if so, the doctor will have to examine the body and arrange for another doctor to do so, too.

laying out the body

You can ask an undertaker to come to take the body away or to lay it out at home; he may charge for this service.

Rigor mortis, a stiffening of the muscles, usually begins within about 6 hours after death, and gradually extends over the whole body in about 18 hours, after which it begins to wear off. Rigor mortis is less pronounced in the body of an old person.

When someone has been dead for about half an hour or more, parts of the skin will have started to discolour. This discoloration, which is called post mortem staining, is caused by the blood sinking under the action of gravity.

Laying out, usually done by a nurse or by one of the undertaker's staff, should be done as soon as possible. The body is washed, the natural orifices stopped up with cotton wool and a napkin, and clean clothes put on. The eyelids are closed and the jaw supported, the hair is tidied and the arms and feet put straight. A man may need to be shaved. When the laying out is done at home, the person laying out usually brings most of the necessary equipment, but may ask to be given a sheet and some towels, a pillow, warm water, soap and disinfectant, and perhaps a nightdress or pyjamas or a shirt to put on the body.

If someone has died quietly and expectedly at home and in bed, it is all right to tidy the room and rearrange or lay out the body. But if you discover a dead body in any other circumstances, do as little as possible to it until the doctor comes. Do not move it unless it is likely to be damaged or cause damage where it is.

calling the police

If you think that death appears to have been caused by an accident or violence, or to have occurred in other non-natural or suspicious circumstances, you should at once inform the police.

Do not touch or move anything in the room, nor allow anyone else to do so, until the police say that you may. The police will almost certainly want to take statements from anyone who was with the deceased when he died, or who discovered the body, but no one is obliged to give a statement to the police. If there is an inquest later, anyone who has made a statement may be called as a witness, as may any person whom the coroner believes may be able to give information about the death.

If a body cannot be immediately identified, the police circulate a description in police journals, and occasionally to the general press, too. Anyone who might be able to identify the body usually has to go to the mortuary with the police.

If the police are called and no relative or other person responsible is immediately available, the police take possession of any cash or valuables. As a general rule, this property is given up to whoever can later prove his right to it. The police also take away any article which may have a bearing on the cause of death – a letter or bottle of pills, for example – in case this is needed by the coroner.

medical certificate of cause of death
The law requires that every death in this country shall be registered. For this, medical evidence of the cause of death must be given. The person who has authority to do so is either the coroner or the doctor who was looking after the deceased during the final illness. More usually, it is the doctor who issues a medical certificate of cause of death. On the medical certificate, the doctor states to the best of his knowledge and belief the cause or causes of death, the last date on which he had seen the deceased alive, and whether or not a doctor has seen the body. The doctor is not allowed to charge for this certificate.

The doctor either gives the certificate to one of the deceased's relatives to take to the registrar of the area in which the death took place or he sends it to the registrar.

registering the death

In this country, deaths should be registered within five days of the death. Registration can be delayed for a further nine days provided the registrar receives, in writing, confirmation that a medical certificate of cause of death has been signed by the doctor.

Under english law, all deaths must be registered in the registration sub-district in which they took place or in which the body was found. A list of names, addresses and telephone numbers of local registrars of birth and deaths is usually displayed in doctors' surgeries, in post offices, and in public libraries and other public buildings, together with their office hours and a description of the sub-district they cover.

Usually, whoever is giving the information goes in person to the registrar's office. Very few registration districts have an appointment system; normally you just go along during the registrar's office hours and wait until he is free to see you.

the informant
The law defines who qualifies to give the required information to the registrar. Attached to the doctor's medical certificate of cause of death is a 'notice to informant', with a list of people who can act as informant.

If the death occurred in a house or inside any other building, the informant can be

○ a relative who was present at the death or during the last illness
○ a relative who lives, or happens to be, in the sub-district of the registrar for the deceased.

If there is no eligible relative, the informant can be

○ any other person who was present at the death
○ the occupier of the house (in a public institution, the senior resident officer)
○ anyone else living in the house who knew about the death
○ the person responsible for making the funeral arrangements.

If the person had been found dead out of doors, the informant could be a relative who has enough information about the deceased to complete the details for the registrar; or anyone who happened to be there when the person died or who found the body; or whoever is responsible for making the funeral arrangements or is in charge of the body (this will be the police if the body cannot be identified).

The responsibility of being an informant must not be delegated to anyone not qualified to act. The doctor when issuing the medical certificate of cause of death should give the 'notice to informant' to the person who is going to be the informant, who should take it to the registrar. If the informant does not have the medical evidence of the cause of death (because the doctor is sending the medical certificate direct to the registrar), he or she should allow time for the evidence to reach the registrar before going to register the death.

If the registrar finds that the information the doctor has been able to give on the medical certificate of cause of death is inadequate, or that the death was due to some reportable cause, he will have to report the death to the coroner and await his written clearance before proceeding with the registration.

procedure

The procedure for registering a death is a simple question-and-answer interview between the registrar and the informant.

The registrar will, first of all, make sure that the death took place in his sub-district; he cannot register a death which occurred in any place outside his jurisdiction. He will ask in what capacity whoever is registering the death qualifies to be the informant – relative, present at the death, or other reason. The registrar may ask if the informant has brought the deceased's birth certificate and marriage certificate, and national health service medical card. It is not essential for him to have these, but they contain some of the information the registrar will need.

Then the registrar fills in a draft form for the register of deaths with the date of death and exactly where it occurred, the sex, names and surname of the dead person. It is as well to give all the names by which the deceased had ever been known, so that there can be no doubt who the particulars refer to. In order to avoid difficulties over identity in connection with probate, insurance policies, pensions and bank accounts, the names should be the same as those on birth and marriage certificates, and on any other relevant documents. The maiden surname of a married woman is required. The date and place of birth of the dead person, and last address are entered. For someone who died away from home, the home address should be given.

Next, the registrar will ask what was the last full-time occupation of the deceased, and whether he or she was retired at the time of death. A woman who was married or widowed at the time of her death would be described as 'wife of' or 'widow of', followed by the name and occupation of her husband, in addition to her own occupation or profession. A woman who had never been married or a woman whose marriage had been dissolved would have her occupation recorded, with no reference to her marital status.

Children under the age of sixteen are described as 'son of' or 'daughter of', followed by the names and occupations of the parents.

The registrar copies the medical cause of death from the doctor's certificate or the coroner's notification, and adds the name and qualification of the doctor or coroner.

On the draft form, but not in the register itself, the registrar enters the deceased's national health service number. If the deceased was over sixteen years old, additional information is requested: marital status at the time of death (single, married, widowed or divorced) and the age of any widow or widower left. This information is not entered in the register in England and Wales, and is used only for the preparation of population statistics by the Registrar General.

The registrar will ask for the deceased's medical card. If the informant has not brought it, the registrar will give him a pre-paid addressed envelope to send it later. This is to enable the national health service register to be kept up to date.

entry in the register

The informant should check the draft of the proposed entry in the register to make sure that there is nothing wrong or misleading in it. When the particulars are agreed, the registrar makes the entry in the register itself and asks the informant to check and sign it. The informant should sign his usual signature, even if this is not his whole name. The registrar has to use special ink for the register, so sign with the pen he offers.

After adding the date of the registration, the registrar himself signs the entry in the final space. Any errors can be corrected without formality before the entry has been signed, but once it is signed by the registrar, the entry cannot be corrected without the authority of the Registrar General, who may require documentary evidence to justify the correction.

The registrar can now let you have copies of the entry in the register (the death certificates) which you may need for probate and other purposes.

Make a note of the number of the entry in the register and the date, and of the registration district, because you may need more copies of the entry later.

FOR REGISTRATION – THE DOCUMENTS

notice to informant	from doctor	gives details of who must register death and what particulars will be required	via relative registrar
medical certificate of cause of death	from doctor	states cause of death	to registrar (direct or vi relative)
if coroner involved: coroner's notification	from coroner	confirms or gives details of cause of death	direct to registrar
or coroner's certificate after inquest	from coroner	gives all the particulars required for death to be registered	direct to registrar

registering a stillbirth

The process of registering a stillbirth is a mixture of registering a birth and registering a death and has to be done within 42 days.

People qualified to register a stillbirth are (as for live births): the mother; the father if the child would have been legitimate had it been born alive; the occupier of the house or other premises in which the stillbirth occurred; a person who was present at the stillbirth or who found the stillborn child.

A stillborn child is a child born after the 28th week of pregnancy which did not at any time after being completely expelled from its mother breathe or show any other signs of life. Foetal death before the 28th week does not fall within the legal definition of a stillbirth and is usually considered a miscarriage. If it occurred in hospital, the hospital will arrange the disposal of the foetus.

If a doctor was in attendance at a stillbirth or examined the body of the stillborn child, he gives a certificate of stillbirth, stating the cause of death and the duration of the pregnancy. A certified midwife can issue the certificate if no doctor was there. If no doctor or midwife was in attendance at, or after, the birth, one of the parents, or some other qualified informant, can make a declaration on a form (form 35, available from the registrar of births and deaths), saying that to the best of his or her knowledge and belief the child was stillborn.

If there is any doubt whether the child was born alive or not, the case must be reported to the coroner of the district, who may then order a post mortem or an inquest and will issue a certificate of the cause of death when he has completed his inquiries.

When registering a stillbirth, the registrar has to have the doctor's or midwife's certificate, or a declaration of the stillbirth. Whoever goes to register has to tell the registrar the name, surname and maiden name of the mother, her place of birth and her usual residence at the time of the child's birth; if she had never been married, also her occupation. If the child would have been legitimate, the name, surname and occupation of the father and his place of birth are required.

If the father and mother are married to each other, the registrar asks the month and year of the marriage, and the number of the mother's previous children, both born alive and stillborn, by her present and any former husband; this information is needed for statistical purposes only in order to forecast population trends and is not entered in the register.

No certified copy of the entry (death certificate) is given from the register of stillbirths unless the Registrar General's express permission has been obtained.

death in hospital

When death has taken place in a hospital or a similar institution, what happens up to the time of registering is slightly different from the arrangements that have to be made if a person has died at home.

The relatives, or whoever was named as 'next of kin' when the patient was admitted, are informed of the death by the ward nursing staff. If death was unexpected or the result of an accident, it may be the police who find and tell the relatives. If the dead person was not already an inpatient at the hospital, a member of the family may be asked to come to identify the body.

Hospitals differ from each other in procedure but it is usually the administrative rather than the medical staff who make the arrangements with the relatives. In most hospitals, one clerk undertakes all the formalities; in some, the relatives may have to deal with several people. If a patient dies out of office hours, an appointment will be made for the relatives to come on the following day to be told about the procedure. Whoever goes to the hospital will be asked to take away the deceased's possessions so it is advisable to take along a suitcase or a large bag. You will probably have to sign a form of receipt for the belongings you take away.

A hospital will not recommend any particular undertaker but should be able to show you a list of names and addresses of undertakers in the area.

The medical certificate of cause of death is usually completed by a hospital doctor. However, if the person had died before a hospital doctor had a chance to diagnose the cause, the dead person's own doctor is asked to issue the medical certificate. If this is not possible, the death will be reported to the coroner. Also a hospital has to report to the coroner a death that took place when the patient was undergoing an operation or before recovering from the effect of anaesthesia. It is usual for all deaths occurring within 24 hours of an operation to be reported. Other circumstances which have to be reported to the coroner include when the death was sudden and unexplained or occurred under suspicious circumstances, or when the death might be due to an industrial disease, to a medical mishap, to an accident, or to violence, neglect, abortion or any kind of poisoning. Once the case is accepted by the coroner, responsibility for the body lies with his office and not the hospital, and the coroner's office not the hospital is where relatives should then seek information. The hospital will tell relatives how to contact the coroner's office.

If the certificate of cause of death can be issued at the hospital and the death is not being reported to the coroner, the family has to arrange for the body to be taken away from the hospital mortuary. A relative or executor will have to sign a form authorising the undertakers to remove the body. If the body is to be cremated, the necessary medical forms will be completed at the hospital; the doctors' charge for this is usually added to the undertaker's bill.

Hospitals often want to carry out a post mortem examination (autopsy) to find out more about the cause of death. The hospital cannot carry out such a post mortem without the permission of the deceased's next of kin. The person who goes to the hospital following a death should therefore be prepared to say whether the next of kin will allow the hospital to carry out a post mortem, and, if so, to sign a consent form. Relatives are told the result of the post mortem, if they want to know.

Relatives may be asked if they have any objections to the use of eyes, kidneys, heart or other organs for transplant surgery. Even if a patient had completed a donor card, it is still likely that the relatives will be asked for their consent before any organs are removed.

The procedure for registering the death is the same as for an ordinary death at home, but the registration must be done at the office of the registrar in whose district the hospital is.

funeral provided

Where there are no relatives or friends to arrange and meet the cost of the funeral, the health authority is empowered to do so. Hospitals have arrangements with local undertakers to provide a simple funeral. Although technically the health authority bears responsibility, in practice the funeral arrangements are made by the staff of the hospital where the patient died.

donated organs for transplant

The removal of organs for transplantation is permitted in law either if the dead person has previously indicated willingness to be a donor, in writing (for example, by signing a donor card), or if after 'reasonable enquiry' there is no reason to believe that the surviving relatives have any objections. The most usual organs to be used in this way are the kidneys, heart, liver, eyes.

If the person who has died had completed a donor card, the next of kin or whoever is in charge of the body at the time of death should, once death has been certified, immediately notify the medical authorities, either through the GP or direct to the nearest hospital. It is essential that the organ to be used is removed as soon after death as possible. Delay means that serious damage may occur and it is therefore usual for kidneys, heart or liver from people dying in hospital as a result of an accident to be used.

After a sudden death, or one following an accident, the next of kin may be asked by the hospital whether they would allow an undamaged organ to be taken for transplant, even though the dead person has not left a request that this be done.

The usual procedure is for the hospital doctor to inform the local transplant centre that an organ for transplant may be available. A member of the transplant service, usually a doctor, will secure the necessary permission from the coroner and arrange for the removal of the organ required. The body is then available to the relatives for burial or cremation in the usual way. There is no disfigurement. If not already in hospital, the body will have to be taken to a hospital for the removal operation.

The process should not delay the funeral arrangements: the death can be registered meanwhile.

eyes

The cornea from the eyes of a dead person can be used to restore sight. There is no upper age limit for donors. The colour of the eyes, sex, race, blood group and tissue type of the donor are irrelevant. Even if glasses were worn this does not affect the acceptability of the corneas.

If the death is being reported to the coroner, the eyes must not be removed without his prior permission.

Corneas do not deteriorate as rapidly as other parts of the body after death so can be removed for grafting up to 12 hours after death, provided that the corneas have not meanwhile been exposed and allowed to dry, but a shorter time is preferable.

The corneas can be removed at home, without the body having to be moved to a hospital. As with any form of organ donation, it may only be carried out where there is no objection from the next of kin.

Until recently, only surgeons were allowed to remove donor eye tissue so if a donor died at home or in a different hospital, a surgeon had to go out and retrieve the valuable corneal tissue. The implementation of the Corneal Transplant Act in August 1986 allows properly qualified technicians to remove corneal tissue. This means that, since there are more technicians than surgeons, a greater number of donated corneas can be retrieved and more corneal transplants carried out.

There is a special corneal transplant service (at present paid for by the Iris Fund for Prevention of Blindness and run as part of the UK transplant service) for taking corneas from donors to the nearest hospital grafting centre or eye bank, with minimal delay.

body donated for medical education or research

A number of people express a wish that their body shall be used after death for medical research and/or education. Bodies donated in this way are used by doctors and by medical students who are studying and researching into the structure and function of the normal human body. Research into specific medical disease is not carried out at these examinations.

If such a wish has been expressed and death occurs in the London area, the next of kin or executor should straight-away telephone the London Anatomy Office (741 2198); out of office hours, the DHSS (407 5522). Elsewhere, the department of anatomy at the nearest medical school should be contacted. In cases of difficulty, get in touch with HM Inspector of Anatomy on 01-703 6380.

If at the time of death a medical school has no need for a body or if death occurs too far away from the medical school to make transporting the body practicable, the donation will be rejected. And a body cannot be accepted if the coroner is involved or if death is the result of certain illness, such as cancer. In only a minority of cases are wishes for anatomical donation actually carried out: post mortem examination and cancer account for half the rejections of proferred bodies. So, until acceptance of the body is confirmed, the family should continue to make arrangements for the funeral, in case the deceased's wishes for the medical use of his body cannot be carried out.

If the body is accepted, arrangements will be made by the medical school immediately for the body to be collected by a firm of funeral directors and transported to the appropriate medical school. In the meantime, the executors or next of kin should obtain the medical certificate from the doctor in charge of the case and register the death as soon as possible.

The green disposal certificate for burial or cremation from the registrar should be sent to the medical school.

The family and executors need make no further arrangements: it is the responsibility of the medical school to arrange and pay for burial or cremation when the time comes. The body will be either buried or cremated according to the wishes of the deceased and next of kin. If the body is eventually to be cremated, the executor may be asked to complete and sign the statutory application form for cremation, or this may be signed by the professor of the medical school.

Unless the next of kin ask to be allowed to make arrangements themselves for a private funeral at their own expense, the medical school arranges and pays for a simple funeral. If instructions have not been given by the person handing over the body that no ceremony be held, a simple service is conducted at the funeral by a minister or priest of the faith professed by the deceased. The medical school does not put up individual headstones.

If burial or cremation in some place other than that normally used by the medical school is requested, or particularly elaborate arrangements, the extra expense must be met by the relatives or executors. Some medical schools give no option on the method or procedure of disposal.

AFTER REGISTRATION

A document which confirms the registration of the death is needed in order to claim the various national insurance benefits after someone has died. The registrar issues this when registering the death. If registration of the death has had to be delayed for any reason, the registrar can issue a certificate of notification of death provided he has received the necessary evidence of death from the doctor or coroner. This certificate of registration or notification is free and is of use only for claiming national insurance benefits. The application form for claiming (form BD8) is printed on the back of the certificate.

death certificates

The certificates you will need when making other arrangements about the deceased's affairs are all certified copies of the entry of death in the register – death certificates. A 'standard' death certificate is the one for sending with an application for a grant of probate or letters of administration.

There is a specific certificate for claiming from a registered friendly society (or the standard death certificate can be used). To obtain this certificate, you must tell the registrar the name of the friendly society concerned. You may not know from the name of the society or company whether it is an industrial assurance company or a friendly society, but if you take the policies or a list of the full titles with you to the registrar, he should be able to tell you.

Neither the standard certificate nor the friendly society certificate will be accepted for claims in connection with insurance taken out on the life of a parent or grandparent by a child, adopted child, stepchild or grandchild. A different special certificate must be obtained for this. On the application form for this certificate, the applicant certifies that he had taken out an insurance on the life of the deceased parent or grandparent and states his relationship. Unlike other death certificates, it is solely for the use of the applicant whose name and address is given. Only one of these special death certificates is issued to any one person. If more than one insurance company is involved, the certificate should be reclaimed after each company has endorsed it. If the original certificate is lost or destroyed, a duplicate can only be obtained if the applicant makes a statutory declaration in front of a JP, magistrate, commissioner for oaths or a practising solicitor.

Yet another form of death certificate is issued for 'certain other statutory purposes' for claiming under various national insurance and social security acts. This death certificate can be used instead of the free certificate of registration of the death (incorporating form BD8) for claiming national insurance benefits, if the BD8 certificate has been lost. In cases where probate is not required, this is the certificate needed for encashing national savings certificates, premium savings bonds, national savings bank deposits at the post office.

If you want the registrar to advise you about the number and type of certificates you may need, take with you a list of the various purposes for which you think some evidence of the death may be required.

DEATH CERTIFICATES (England and Wales)

	cost from registrar	purpose
certificate of registration/ notification of death (incorporating form BD8)	free	for claiming death grant and widow's benefit from the Department of Health and Social Security
standard death certificate	£2	for obtaining probate; for private claims such as life insurance and pension schemes; also for registered friendly societies
special death certificate	£1.50	for claiming insurance taken out on the life of a parent or grandparent
certificate for purposes of friendly societies acts	£1.50	for claiming from a registered friendly society
certificate for certain statutory purposes	£1.50	for claiming under the national insurance and social security acts, or if the certificate of registration of death has been lost; when probate is not required, for claiming on national savings banks, national savings certificates and premium savings bonds

getting death certificates later

You can get further copies of certificates for £2 while that volume of the death register remains with the registrar who registered the death.

When the local registrar's volume of a death register is filled, it is passed to the superintendent registrar of the district, who can issue death certificates if you need them later on. The cost of a standard certificate from a superintendent registrar is £5.

If the death was registered more than about a year previously, standard death certificates can also be obtained from the General Register Office, St Catherines House, 10 Kings-way, London WC2B 6JP. The charge is £5 if you go in person to St Catherines House; £10 if you apply by post.

If you need to apply for certificates from the registrar of another district, your local registrar can tell you the names and addresses of all other registrars. He can give you the application forms needed for the various certificates and help you to complete them. With any postal application for a certificate, you must send the necessary cheque or postal order and a stamped addressed envelope. When you get certificates from a registrar in person, you are expected to pay there and then.

In Northern Ireland, the General Register Office address is Oxford House, 49–55 Chichester Street, Belfast BT1 4HL, and the charge for a standard death certificate is £3.75. The special death certificates for insurance purposes cost £1.25.

For registering a death and getting death certificates in Scotland, see pages 46 to 48.

THE CORONER

The office of the coroner was instituted in England in norman times. He was the king's officer appointed for a shire or a borough for the purpose of keeping an eye on the sheriff, keeping a record of all sudden deaths (that is, deaths which were 'against the course of nature') and of any occurrence by which monies or property might be forfeit and revert to the crown.

Nowadays the coroner is a qualified doctor or lawyer, sometimes both. He is paid by the local authority but is independent of both local and central government and is responsible only to the Crown. His duties include instituting inquiries regarding the finding of any gold or silver whose ownership is unknown in order to discover whether it is treasure trove and therefore belongs to the Crown. His main function, however, is to investigate any death which has been reported to him.

deaths to be reported to the coroner

A death has to be reported by a doctor to the coroner if the doctor had not attended the deceased at all during his last illness. Even if the doctor had been treating the patient, if he had not seen him within the last 14 days, the death will have to be reported to the coroner. (In Northern Ireland, the period within which the doctor should have last seen the patient is 28 days.)

A death attributable to what is classified as an industrial disease and in some cases one caused or accelerated by an injury received during military service, however long ago, must be reported to the coroner.

Other circumstances in which a death must be reported to the coroner include when death

○ was sudden and unexplained
○ occurred in suspicious circumstances
○ was caused directly or indirectly by any kind of accident
○ might have been due to
   neglect
   any kind of poisoning
   dependence on or abuse of drugs
   abortion
○ was suicide
○ occurred while in prison or in police custody
○ took place during a surgical operation or before recovery from the effects of anaesthesia.

reporting death to the coroner

Anyone who is uneasy about the apparent cause of a death has the right to inform the coroner for the district. By telephoning a police station, you can find out who is the relevant coroner and how to get in touch with him. The telephone number of the coroner's court is in the telephone directory under 'courts'. Or you can give information to any local police station, who will pass the information to the coroner's officer, who is almost always a police officer.

The information does not have to be an allegation of some crime. There may be some circumstances which you feel are contributory to the death but may not have been known to the doctor – such as an old war wound or injury – which can be established by a post mortem examination. If you believe that the deceased may have died from some industrial disease, it is obviously best to inform the coroner before the person is cremated, otherwise the matter can never be resolved.

Generally, however, it is the doctor who reports a death to the coroner, or the police. Medical certificates of cause of death carry a list of the types of case that the doctor should report to the coroner. If the death comes within this category, the usual practice is for the doctor to inform the coroner directly, before anyone has gone to register the death.

It may be that the registrar, when he gets the doctor's medical certificate of the cause of death, decides that because of the cause or circumstances of the death, he must report the death to the coroner. In such a case, there will be a delay before the death can be registered, which may interfere with the arrangements that the family had hoped to make for the funeral.

The coroner may decide that there is no need for further investigation, being satisfied that the cause of death is known to be natural, and that the death can be registered from the certificate provided by the doctor. In this case, the coroner sends a formal notice of his decision to the registrar of the district, and the death can then be registered in the usual way by the qualified informant.

If the registrar knows who the next of kin are, he gets in touch with them and tells them that he is now in a position to register the death. If the death had been reported to the coroner direct and the registrar does not know who the next of kin are, they will have to find out from the coroner's office when to go to the registrar.

coroner's investigations

If the coroner decides that the death must be investigated further, the death cannot be registered until a certificate is provided by the coroner when he has completed his inquiries. But the coroner can issue an interim certificate of death, which is usually adequate for starting to deal with the estate of the deceased.

The funeral will have to await the outcome of his investigations. The coroner's office may be able to advise the family when the body will be released and when the forms will be available for the family to plan the funeral.

In the majority of cases, the coroner's involvement is a formality and reporting a death to the coroner does not inevitably mean a post mortem or an inquest. It is up to each individual coroner to decide what action shall be taken.

post mortem
The majority of post mortem examinations are ordered by the coroner to establish the cause of death. This may be to show that the death was a natural one or it may resolve a dispute where the family might believe that the death was caused by an industrial disease (a person may have suffered from an industrial illness in life but die from some other, unrelated, cause). In a few cases, the post mortem provides valuable evidence of the manner of a criminal death.

The coroner orders a post mortem if the law requires this. The family of the deceased do not have to be asked to give their consent, as they would be when a hospital wants to perform a post mortem examination. The coroner arranges and pays for the post mortem.

If a family object to a post mortem examination for religious or other reasons, or if they have any reason to believe that the examination is not necessary, they should inform the coroner. If the coroner is still of the opinion that the examination is required, the family can make an application to the High Court to reverse the decision of the coroner. This will delay arrangements for the disposal of the body.

If the post mortem reveals that the death was due to a natural cause and no other circumstance warrants further investigation, the coroner notifies the registrar and the death can be registered in the usual way. In some districts, the coroner's officer or another policeman calls on the family to tell them; otherwise, the next of kin should enquire at the coroner's office every few days to find out when the coroner's notification is being sent to the registrar. The coroner has no duty to inform the next of kin of the result of the post mortem.

After the post mortem, the body becomes again the responsibility of the family. To avoid unnecessary delays, the family can arrange for an undertaker to collect the necessary forms from the coroner's office as soon as these are available and make arrangements for the funeral at the earliest suitable date.

inquest

The coroner is obliged to hold an inquest into every violent and unnatural death that is reported to him, and also following the death of a person in prison.

An inquest is an inquiry to determine who the deceased person was, and how, when and where that person died, and to establish the particulars that are required for the registration of the death.

An inquest is held formally and is open to the public. A person wishing to attend, but who has not been given notice of the inquest, can ask at a local police station or telephone the coroner's office to find out when the inquest is being held. The coroner may have asked for further investigations and tests to be carried out, and the date for the inquest will not be arranged until these are all complete.

at the court

The coroner's court is a court of law with power to summon witnesses and jurors, and with power to deal with any contempt in the face of the court.

The law requires that any person with evidence to give concerning the death should attend an inquest. In practice, the coroner will have read any written statements that have been made, and will know the names of those who have been interviewed by the police and by his officers. The witnesses the coroner knows will be needed are summoned to the inquest. The summons is often an informal telephone call but there may be a written summons or a subpoena (if the witness is outside the jurisdiction of the coroner). A witness is entitled to travel expenses and to a fixed sum to compensate for loss of earnings.

If any witnesses know that they cannot attend, they should inform the coroner's office at once. When a witness has been formally summoned, there are penalties for failing to attend. Non-attendance causes inconvenience, and expense to the family if the inquest has to be adjourned.

Unlike a trial, there are no 'sides' at an inquest. Anyone who is regarded as having a proper interest may ask witnesses questions at an inquest and may be legally represented. The list of people with a 'proper interest' includes parents, children and spouse of the deceased, insurers and beneficiaries of an insurance policy on the life of the deceased, any person whose conduct is called into question regarding the cause of the death, and, in appropriate cases, a chief officer of police, government inspector, trade union official.

There is a minimum amount of pomp and ceremony at an inquest. The coroner calls witnesses in turn from the main part of the court to come up to the witness box. Each witness swears or affirms that he will 'speak the truth, the whole truth and nothing but the truth'.

First, the coroner questions the witness; then, with his permission, the witness can be examined by anyone present who has a proper interest in the case (or by that person's legal representative). If you know that you will want to give evidence or examine a witness, tell the coroner's officer beforehand, so that the coroner can call you at the right moment.

When all the witnesses have been heard, the coroner sums up (there are no speeches by the lawyers) and gives his verdict.

with a jury

Some inquests have to be heard before a jury. The jury is summoned in the same way as a crown court jury. In cases of industrial accidents or other incidents that must be reported to a government department, after a death in prison or in police custody or caused by the act of a police officer, and where death was in circumstances that present a danger to the public, there is always a jury.

The jury for an inquest consists of not less than 7 and not more than 11 men or women eligible for jury service. There is not the power to challenge jurors – there is no accused person to exercise the power. The jurors are on oath. Jurors need not view the body unless the coroner directs them to.

At the conclusion of his inquiries, the coroner sums up the evidence to the jury and explains the law. All the findings of the inquest are then made by the jury. Jurors do not usually leave the court to discuss their decision but may do so. They can return a majority verdict.

the verdict

The purpose of an inquest is not only to find out who the deceased person was and how, when and where he came by his death, but also to decide the category of death. This is colloquially called the verdict but the correct description is the conclusion. It can range from natural causes to suicide, industrial disease, unlawful killing. Conclusions are subject to many legal technicalities. In particular, the finding of suicide must be strictly proved: when there is no conclusive evidence of the intent to commit suicide, the coroner has to return an open verdict.

The conclusion must not appear to determine any matter of criminal liability against a named person, nor any matter of civil liability.

A verdict of accidental death does not mean that there will be no prosecution in a magistrates' court or that the family cannot bring an action for damages. All it means is that it is not a case of suicide or homicide. The 'properly interested persons' are entitled to a copy of the notes of the evidence and these are often useful in subsequent proceedings.

inquest adjourned
The coroner can adjourn any inquest at his own discretion – for instance, to await the result of an inquiry into an air crash or other disaster. The coroner can provide any properly interested person with an interim certificate of the fact of death. This will allow any insurance or other payments to be claimed and the estate to be administered.

An inquest has to be adjourned where a person has been charged with causing the death, or with an offence connected with the death that will be the subject of a trial before a crown court jury. The coroner opens the inquest by taking evidence of the identity of the deceased and the medical cause of death. The inquest is then adjourned. (In a very few cases, the inquest may be resumed after the trial.) Within 5 days of adjourning an inquest, the coroner must send to the registrar a certificate giving the particulars required for the death to be registered.

the press and inquests
Since inquests are held in public, the press can be present. There are restrictions on the publication of the names of minors, but in other matters there are no reporting restrictions.

Death is always a sensational subject. Although the coroner may try to choose words carefully, people giving evidence or questioning witnesses may provide comments that can be distressing to the family. The coroner will try to ensure that the facts are as accurate as possible; the inquest may be able to dispel rumours and inaccurate assertions.

the cost
There should be no expense to the family arising out of an inquest. Representation by a lawyer is not necessary in the majority of inquests, and in cases where there is no controversy, the family should not make an unnecessary expenditure at such a time. There is no provision for representation at an inquest under the legal aid scheme.

Many people think it wise, however, to be represented by a solicitor at the inquest in the case of death resulting from an accident or an occupational disease, because there may be compensation claims to be made later and a solicitor would be better able to make use of the evidence presented at an inquest. Someone who does not know of a solicitor can go to a citizens advice bureau, who can arrange a free or small-fee interview with a lawyer. The CAB will ensure that a family who has just lost the person providing their income do not pay out money unnecessarily, and may also advise on any prospect of some compensation.

after the inquest
In all cases other than those involving a serious crime, registration of the death takes place when the coroner sends

a certificate after inquest to the registrar of births and deaths of the district in which the death took place or in which the body was found. This certificate provides the registrar with the information he needs to register the death. No informant is required to attend the registrar's office. The death certificates can be obtained by the family from the registrar any time after the inquest.

DEATH REPORTED TO CORONER

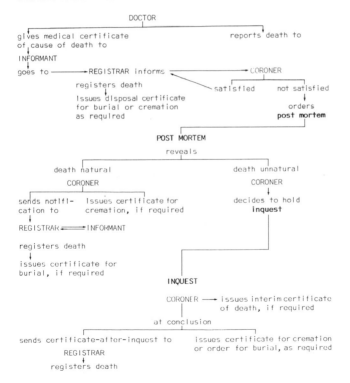

certificate for burial or cremation

Once a death has been registered, the registrar issues a green certificate, referred to generally as the disposal certificate, authorising either burial or application for cremation. A body cannot be buried or cremated without this certificate or its equivalent – namely, the coroner's order for burial or certificate for cremation. It is unwise to make more than provisional arrangements for the funeral until you have the certificate from the registrar or the coroner. You will get a burial or cremation certificate from the registrar or from the coroner but not from both.

The registrar can issue a certificate before registering a death but only when he has already received the requisite information (including medical evidence) and is just waiting for the informant to come and register the death. This may arise, for instance, when the only suitable informant is ill in hospital but the funeral has to take place. A certificate issued by the registrar before registration authorises burial only; crematorium authorities are not allowed to accept such a certificate.

If the death has been reported to the coroner and he has ordered a post mortem examination, only he can authorise cremation; if the body is to be buried, the registrar can issue the burial certificate. If there has been an inquest, it is the coroner who issues either an order for burial or a certificate for cremation.

No fee is charged for a registrar's certificate or coroner's order. If you lose it, you (or the undertaker) have to apply to the registrar or the coroner who issued the original certificate for a duplicate.

Once you have obtained the necessary certificate from the registrar or the coroner, give it to the undertaker who will take it to the church, cemetery or crematorium officials.

Without it, they will not bury or cremate a body. It is the responsibility of the church, cemetery or crematorium to complete part C of the certificate and to return it to the registrar confirming disposal has taken place. If the registrar does not receive part C within 14 days of the certificate having been issued, he will get in touch with the person to whom the certificate had been given to find out what is happening.

SCOTLAND

The medical certificate of cause of death given by doctors in Scotland is similar to that in England. The obligation to give the certificate rests on the doctor who attended the deceased during his last illness but, if there was no doctor in attendance, the certificate may be issued by any doctor who is able to do so. The doctor hands the certificate to a relative to take to the local registrar or sends it direct to the registrar. In the majority of cases, the certificate is issued to a relative.

If a medical certificate of cause of death cannot be given, the registrar can, nevertheless, register the death but must report the facts of the case to the procurator fiscal.

the procurator fiscal

There are no coroners in Scotland and the duties which in England would be carried out by a coroner are in Scotland carried out by a procurator fiscal. The procurator fiscal is a full-time law officer, who comes under the Lord Advocate.

The procurator fiscal has many functions, including responsibility for investigating all unexpected and violent deaths and also any death which occurred under suspicious circumstances. If he is satisfied with the doctor's medical certificate and any evidence he receives from the police, he need take no further action. If, however, the procurator fiscal considers a further medical report is necessary, he requests a medical practitioner (frequently a police surgeon) to report to him 'on soul and conscience' what he considers was the cause of death.

post mortem

In the majority of cases, a post mortem is not carried out and the doctor certifies the cause of death after an external examination.

The mere fact that the cause of death is in a medical sense unexplained is not a ground for ordering a dissection at the public expense, provided the intrinsic circumstances sufficiently explain the cause of death in a popular sense and do not raise a suspicion of criminality or negligence.

In cases where the procurator fiscal decides a post mortem is necessary, permission to carry it out is given by the sheriff. One doctor is usually sufficient but if, while conducting the dissection, the doctor finds unexpected difficulties, the procurator fiscal may decide to bring in a second doctor. Where there is a possibility of criminal proceedings being taken against someone and it is necessary to prove the fact and cause of death, a post mortem should be carried out by two medical practitioners.

public inquiry
Death while in legal custody or as the result of an accident during work must be the subject of a public inquiry, which takes the place of an inquest in England. If a person, while engaged in industrial employment or occupation, died of natural causes, there may, but will not necessarily, be a public inquiry.

The procurator fiscal has to report certain cases to the Crown Office and it is the Lord Advocate who makes the final decision about whether to apply to a sheriff for an inquiry to be held. In all other cases, investigations made into sudden deaths are carried out by the procurator fiscal confidentially.

Before reporting a case to the Crown Office, the procurator fiscal interviews witnesses and the relatives in private (this is called a precognition).

Cases which are reported to the Crown Office because they may result in a public inquiry are essentially those involving a matter of the public interest – for instance, to prevent a recurrence of similar circumstances. Deaths which are directly or indirectly connected with the action of a third party, such as road traffic deaths, may be reported to the Crown Office for consideration either of criminal proceedings or of a public inquiry.

A public inquiry is heard before the sheriff in the local sheriff court. The procurator fiscal examines the witnesses but it is the sheriff who determines the circumstances of the death.

When the investigations are completed, the procurator fiscal notifies the result of his findings to the Registrar General. If the death has already been registered, the Registrar General lets the local registrar know if any changes need to be made to the entry. If the death has not already been registered, the Registrar General instructs the registrar of the district in which the death occurred to register the death.

registering the death

In Scotland, the law requires that every death must be registered within 8 days from the date of death.

The person qualified to act as informant for registering a death is any relative of the deceased, any person present at the death, the deceased's executor or other legal representative, the occupier of the premises where the death took place, or any person having knowledge of the particulars to be registered.

Whereas in England a death mut be registered in the registration office for the district in which the death occurred, in Scotland the death may be registered either in the office for the district in which the death occurred or in the office for the district in which the deceased had normally resided before his death, provided this was also in Scotland. The death of a visitor to Scotland must be registered where the death took place.

As in England, the procedure for registering a death is a simple question-and-answer interview between registrar and informant. The registrar will demand the production of a medical certificate of cause of death or, failing that, the name and address of a doctor who can be asked to give the certificate. The information required by a scottish registrar to register a death is much the same as in England

and Wales, except that he also needs to know the time of death; if the deceased had ever been married, the name, surname and occupation of each spouse; the name and occupation of the deceased's father and the name and maiden surname of the mother, and whether the parents are alive or dead.

When the form of particulars has been completed, the registrar asks the informant to read it over carefully to ensure that all the particulars are correct, and to sign it. The registrar then makes the entry in the register and asks the informant to check it carefully and sign the entry before he adds the date and his own signature.

registering a stillbirth

A stillbirth in Scotland must be registered within 21 days. As in England, if no doctor or midwife can issue a certificate of stillbirth, an informant must make a declaration on a special form. In Scotland, this is form 7, obtainable from the registrar. All such cases, and any case where there is doubt as to whether the child was alive or not, are reported to the procurator fiscal who notifies the Registrar General of the results of his investigations.

If the body is to be cremated, a certificate of stillbirth must be given by the doctor who was in attendance at the confinement (or who conducted a post mortem). The stillbirth must have been registered before cremation can take place.

A stillbirth can be registered either in the district in which it took place or in the district in Scotland in which the mother of the stillborn child was ordinarily resident at the time of the stillbirth.

The informant must produce to the registrar a doctor's or midwife's certificate, or the completed form 7, and is required to give the same information as in England and, in addition, the time of the stillbirth and, where applicable, the place of the parents' marriage.

certificate of registration

There is no direct equivalent in Scotland of a disposal certificate. After registration, the registrar issues to the informant a certificate of registration of death, which should be given to the undertaker to give to the keeper of the burial ground or to the crematorium authorities. There is no charge for this certificate.

death certificates

As in England, the registrar issues, free of charge, a certificate of registration of death which can be used for national insurance purposes only. All other death certificates must be paid for.

The full copy of an entry in the death register (the standard death certificate) costs £2 if applied for within one month of the date of registration. If applied for at a later date, the charge is £5. Each further copy of the same entry ordered at the same time costs £2.50.

The other death certificates cost the same as in England. There are a number of different certificates for various special purposes similar to those in England.

Death certificates are always obtainable from the registrar of the district where the death was registered; they are also obtainable from the General Register Office for Scotland, New Register House, Edinburgh EH1 3YT, at any time after about a year to 18 months from the date of registration. The same fees are charged whether the application is made personally or by post.

DECISIONS ABOUT THE FUNERAL

If the deceased has left no specific instructions, the decision whether to bury or cremate the body is normally made by the executor or the next of kin. If there is neither, the person entrusted by the hospital or local authority to deal with the funeral arrangements has to decide about the disposal of the body. Although it is usual to carry out any wishes the deceased had expressed about the disposal of his body, there is no legal obligation to do so.

Whether the body is to be buried or cremated, many of the arrangements can be made by an individual on his own. But it is rare for a funeral to be carried out without the services of an undertaker.

undertakers

The trade of undertaking started as a comprehensive business some 200 years ago when, in towns, some carpenters began to specialise in the production of coffins and some carriage proprietors in providing funeral carriages. Gradually, these functions merged and developed until the 'undertaking' of a funeral and its arrangements became a separate trade. The status of undertakers was strengthened in the victorian era by the fashion for elaborate, often ostentatious, funerals.

Undertakers have now adopted the title of funeral director and there is a National Association of Funeral Directors (57 Doughty Street, London WC1N 2NE). Members of the NAFD undertake to observe a code of practice drawn up in consultation with the Office of Fair Trading. This includes giving full information about services and prices, providing a written estimate of all charges and a detailed account, offering a basic simple funeral if required. The code also covers general and professional conduct, including confidentiality and the procedure for complaints.

The funeral director's purpose is to assume total responsibility for organising and supplying the necessities for a funeral. The transaction is a business deal and, even though it may be difficult for the next of kin or executor to be businesslike in the circumstances, it should be treated as such, hard-hearted though it may seem.

The family should agree who is to be in charge of and supervise the arrangements: it is not part of an executor's formal duty to be responsible for arranging the funeral.

cost of the funeral

At the time of asking a funeral director to quote, you should have a fairly clear idea of what kind of funeral is wanted and how much can be spent on it. Some people insure during their lifetime for their funeral, or join one of the special friendly societies which pay out a lump sum on death. A funeral director may ask whether the deceased was insured in this way; he then has a better idea of how much the funeral should come to. But usually the cost of a funeral is paid out of the deceased's estate – the money and property he left.

If you intend to spend no more than a limited sum, tell the funeral director and ask what he is prepared to provide for that figure. Do not be persuaded into anything you do not really want, even if he assures you that everyone else has this or that. The funeral director is in business and is justified in trying to sell as many of his services as he can.

You can have preliminary discussions with an undertaker on the telephone, but to conclude the arrangements, he generally comes to you or you have to go to his office. Wherever you see him, the undertaker should show you a price list for the types of funeral he can provide. Ask for a little time on your own to study this and perhaps discuss alternatives with the family and decide what extras you want him to organise by way of transport, flowers, notices, catering.

An undertaker will arrange the funeral for a stillborn child without any ceremony, for an inclusive charge. The hospital or midwife may offer to have arrangements made on the parents' behalf, free of charge.

Funeral directors who are members of the National Federation of Funeral Directors all have to provide what is called a basic funeral, if requested. The lowest prices for a basic simple funeral start at not much less than £350. This includes only the bare minimum: a coffin, a hearse and one following car up to a stated mileage, the bearers to carry the coffin, the services of an undertaker. There is no breakdown given of the cost of these basic services, which each funeral director assesses according to his own overheads and profit margin.

It is as well to be aware of what services the undertaker is supplying for the stated price, and how much any additional items would cost.

coffin

The price quoted for a complete funeral is based on the type of coffin. If you choose one of the more expensive coffins, you will get a more elaborate standard of funeral. Different firms include different items in their inclusive charge.

A funeral director should be able to show you illustrations of the different coffins and caskets he can supply.

A casket is rectangular, instead of the traditional tapered

shape of a coffin. It is usually more expensive than a coffin. The wood affects the price: veneered chipboard is cheapest and japanese oak the most expensive.

The linings of coffins, and other fittings such as pillows and handles, vary considerably according to the price of the coffin. Handles can be expensive, especially if made of brass, and are in many cases ornamental and not used for carrying the coffin (except at jewish funerals).

Many undertakers buy plain coffins from a wholesaler or coffin-maker and keep their own stock of handles, linings and other fittings, which they fix to each coffin when it is ordered. A nameplate will be put on the coffin when the body is in it, giving the name, the date of death and the age of the deceased.

For cremation, it is usual to have a simple and unadorned coffin, with handles and fittings not made of metal. It should therefore be at the cheap end of the price range. It is sometimes covered with a pall throughout the funeral.

other costs

A funeral often involves costs not covered by the funeral director's basic price for a funeral: laying out the body, removing the body from the house or hospital to the undertaker's premises (extra if the removal has to be done outside normal working hours), a shroud or robe, extra cars and additional mileage if the hearse or cars have to go beyond the funeral director's mileage limit. If there is an extra journey – to take the coffin to a church the night before the funeral, for example, or to fetch the body from the mortuary after a post mortem – there will be an extra charge.

All members of the National Association of Funeral Directors must give an itemised written estimate of costs, and most will provide a formal confirmation of funeral arrangements. Even if you 'leave it to him', you should get from the funeral director an estimate of the likely cost.

Church, cemetery or cremation fees have to be paid on top of the undertaker's charge, as do all other payments such as fees for clergyman and organist.

Undertakers ought to be able to tell you charges and conditions of the different churches, cemeteries and crematoria in the area. When comparing the scales of charges in the district, remember that undertakers' charges increase with the distance the funeral has to go.

Generally, the total cost of a funeral, including burial or cremation fees, is unlikely to come to less than about £500, and can be much more. The price levels vary between different parts of the country (for instance, prices tend to be higher in London and the south), as well as varying between local firms.

municipal funerals

A number of local authorities are looking into the possibility of a municipal funeral service. This would be done by arranging with local funeral directors for a simple, low-cost funeral to be available for residents of the local authority area.

The London boroughs of Lambeth and Lewisham already operate such a scheme, and the cost is about half that of an average local funeral.

help with funeral costs

When someone dies who has either no relatives or no one able to pay for the funeral, the London borough or district council of the area where the person died or where the body was found has to arrange the funeral, and if necessary to pay the costs. If the police have a body in their charge for which they cannot trace any relative, they notify the local authority who then have to arrange the funeral. Most local authorities have a contract with a local undertaker for a very simple funeral.

No arrangements should be made by anyone with an undertaker before getting in touch with the local authority social services or environmental health department. Local authorities have no power to reimburse costs where a third party has already arranged a funeral. The local authority may recoup the funeral costs from the deceased's estate or from anyone who was liable to maintain the deceased.

Where someone entitled to supplementary benefit is responsible for arranging the funeral of a relative or member of the same household who was ordinarily resident in the UK prior to the death, but cannot afford to pay for the funeral, it may be possible for some of the cost to be claimed from the supplementary benefits scheme. The costs that may be paid include a plain coffin, transport for coffin and bearers, one car, and the fees for a simple funeral; necessary documentation, some flowers, transporting the body home within this country if he died away from home; and up to £75 of costs arising from a particular requirement of the deceased's religion. An adjudication officer at the social security office should be asked for advice and help over claiming.

Under new legislation from April 1987 some changes are proposed in the criteria and method of payment of a state-funded grant for reasonable funeral expenses.

BURIAL

Arrangements for the funeral can be made but should not be confirmed before the disposal certificate from the registrar, or coroner's order for burial, has been issued; this has to be given to the funeral director.

burial in churchyards

Anyone, whether christian or not, whose permanent address is within the ecclesiastical parish is in theory entitled to be buried in the parish churchyard, even if he dies away from the parish. In practice, there may be no space left in the churchyard. Many old churchyards are closed for further burials, but some churches have burial grounds separated from the church, where parishioners have the right of burial. Ex-parishioners and non-parishioners with family graves or whose close relatives have been buried in the churchyard have the right of burial there, as does anyone who dies within the parish.

It is the incumbent (vicar, rector or priest in charge) and his parochial church council who decide whether to allow someone who has no right by law or custom of burial in the churchyard to be buried there, and what fee to charge. For a non-parishioner, or someone with no connection with the parish, the charges are likely to be higher than for a parishioner.

burial fees

For parishioners. the charges that are payable to the incumbent, to church officials and to the parochial church council for funeral services and burial in Church of England parishes are specified in the Parochial Fees Order. Under the current Parochial Fees Order, the fees payable for a burial (excluding digging charges) with a service beforehand in church come to £36 (proposed increase from 1 January 1987 to £39). Any payment to organist, choir or other musicians is additional; so is extra heating. The fee for burial in a churchyard without having had a service in a church of the parish beforehand is £24 (proposed increase to £27). There is no burial fee for a stillborn infant.

If the parish has its own gravedigger, he will dig the grave for a fee which the vicar lays down. Otherwise, the undertaker has to hire a gravedigger.

the grave
Paying a burial fee does not buy the right to choose the location of the grave in the churchyard. The vicar allots the site. Nor does the burial fee entitle you to ownership of the grave or to the exclusive right of burial in that grave.

by faculty
If you want the exclusive use of a plot in a churchyard, you must apply to the diocesan registrar to reserve a grave space, by a licence called a faculty. Although a faculty gives the right to say who can be buried in the plot, the freehold of the ground continues to belong to the church.

The fee charged by the diocese for a faculty depends on the amount of work involved in the petition. It takes about six weeks for a faculty to be granted. When a person dies, it is too late to get a faculty for him but his relatives could apply for a faculty to reserve the grave for other members of the family. Anyone arranging a burial in a grave reserved by a faculty must produce the faculty or other evidence which proves his right to the grave.

The incumbent charges a fee for the first and each subsequent interment in a grave reserved by faculty. An additional charge is made for removing and replacing an existing headstone to enable subsequent interments in a grave to take place.

burial inside a church
Today, any rights an incumbent may have had in the past to consent to a burial inside his church building have become obsolete. Faculties to permit such burials are hardly ever granted and in urban areas burial in and under a church is prohibited by law.

burial in cemeteries

Most cemeteries are non-denominational, and run either by a local authority or by a privately-owned company. A few cemeteries are owned by a particular denomination; these are generally restricted to members of that faith.

Some cemeteries have a section of the ground consecrated by the Church of England. The fee payable under the Parochial Fees Order to a Church of England clergyman for performing a service in the consecrated part of a cemetery in his parish if there has not been a service in church immediately beforehand is currently £18 (proposed increase on 1 January 1987 to £19.50). There is no fee if the burial immediately follows a prior church service. From 1 January 1987, a fee of £6.50 may be payable to a clergyman for a service of burial in a consecrated part of a cemetery on a separate occasion.

Some cemeteries have ground dedicated to or reserved for other specific religious denominations, and a separate section of general ground. In most cemeteries, any type of religious service (or none at all) can be held. Most cemeteries have a chapel which is nondenominational, and some provide a roster of clergy of different denominations.

fees

Fees for burial in a cemetery vary widely even within the same locality. They are set by the owners, under the terms of the appropriate acts of parliament. Fees and regulations are usually displayed at the cemetery. If you write to the superintendents of the local cemeteries, you will be sent lists or brochures, from which you can compare the charges and conditions. A cemetery's fee may include the services of a clergyman; some will not allow flowers to be planted or put on graves; others will not permit any monument or memorial to be put up, except over the more expensive graves or for only a limited number of years after which the cemetery authorities can remove it. Conditions or payments for maintenance are often stipulated.

In most local authority cemeteries, a higher fee is asked or an additional charge is made for non-residents and non-ratepayers; there may be some concessions for former residents and their relatives. Interment fees are less for children than for adults; each cemetery authority defines its own age limits.

Most local authority cemeteries have an application form which the executor or next of kin usually has to sign. All fees have to be paid in advance, and all the required documents sent to the cemetery a stipulated time before the funeral. This will normally be undertaken by the funeral director.

graves

In most cemeteries, there are various categories of grave.

The cheapest are graves without the right to exclusive burial. The person paying the interment fee has no right to say who else may or may not be buried in the grave. The graves are marked by a number; it may be possible to put up a small memorial or plaque. In some cemeteries, no interments will take place in such a grave for a set number of

years – usually 7 or 14 – after the last burial, except t
there another member of the same family.

In a few cemeteries, for a small fee a grave space can be reserved for a specified period of years from the date of payment. After this, it reverts to the cemetery unless a further fee has been paid either to reserve the space for a further period or for the exclusive right to the grave on behalf of the person buried in it, so that it becomes similar to a private (or purchased) grave.

In most cemeteries, you can buy the right of exclusive burial in a particular plot, in a similar way as by a faculty granted for a grave in a churchyard. The right used to be in perpetuity, but nowadays it is more usually granted for a specific number of years – for instance, 50 or 75.

For a private grave, you get a deed of grant (sometimes referred to as a certificate of ownership), for which some cemeteries make a small charge. The deed should be kept somewhere safe and the family or executors should know where it is. It may have to be produced in evidence before the grave can be opened for an interment. Usually the signature of the owner of the grave is required on the cemetery's application form to authorise the opening of a private grave. If the owner of the exclusive right of burial has died, the cemetery will probably require some alternative formality to authorise the use of the grave if the right had not been re-registered following the death of the owner. Afterwards, the deed will be endorsed with details of the burial and returned to the executors. An interment fee has to be paid in addition, and also a fee for removing and replacing an existing headstone.

Another category of grave is the so-called lawn grave, in which you have the right to exclusive burial but can put up only a very simple headstone, leaving the rest of the grave grass. These graves are always together in one part of the cemetery. You pay less for this type of grave because it is easy to keep lawn graves tidy by mowing them all together. Again, the interment fee is additional. You may not find lawn graves specified as such in a cemetery's list of charges and may have to ask whether there are any lawn graves.

On the plan of a cemetery, the various categories of grave are shown (often by different colours), and you can find from this plan which graves are available at the time.

The fees depend on the type, the size and the depth of the grave and, for a private or a lawn grave, also on its position (in other words, how accessible it is).

A grave which is not lined but is cut into the earth without side support is called an earth grave. A brick grave has a bricked (or concrete) floor and walls and is more expensive than an earth one. For a brick grave, you must have the exclusive right in the grave. Some cemeteries charge a higher interment fee for a brick than for an earth grave and require longer notice for the burial. Formalities and the construction of a brick grave can take weeks.

The standard size of a single grave varies slightly from cemetery to cemetery and a grave larger than the standard size costs more. What is listed as a vault is in some cemeteries a bricked double grave, in others a grave bricked right up to the level of the ground instead of to the top of the coffin.

other burial grounds

If you want to be buried in ground other than a churchyard or cemetery, the law stipulates that such private burials must be registered. Even if you are the freeholder of the land, you must ascertain from the deeds whether the land is restricted in the use to which it may be put. If you want to bury someone in your garden, you must apply for and obtain permission from your local planning authority, and the local environmental health department must be notified and given the opportunity to object to the proposal.

FOR BURIAL – THE DOCUMENTS

registrar's certificate for burial (the disposal certificate) or after inquest:	from registrar	required before burial can take place	via relative and undertaker to burial authorities; part C returns to registrar
coroner's order for burial	from coroner	authorises burial	
application for burial in cemetery	from cemetery via undertaker, usually signed by executor or next of kin	applies for burial and confirms arrangements	to cemetery authorities
grave deeds or faculty	from cemetery or diocese	proves right to grave	to burial authorities
copy of entry in burial register	from burial authorities	proves burial and locates grave	to executor or next of kin

CREMATION

No one can be cremated unless the cause of death has been definitely ascertained. This means that, unlike burial which can be carried out on the authority of a disposal certificate issued before registration, cremation cannot normally be applied for until after the death has been registered and the registrar's certificate issued or a coroner's certificate for cremation given.

the formalities

Before cremation can take place, four statutory forms have to be completed, one by the next of kin, the others by three different doctors. The forms are issued by the crematorium; funeral directors, as a rule, have a supply of them.

Form A is the application for cremation, and has to be completed by the executor, or next of kin, and counter-signed by a householder who knows him personally.

Forms B and C are on the same piece of paper. B has to be completed by the doctor who attended the deceased during the last illness and who has to see the body before he can complete the form. The doctor may have to ask the relatives, or whoever was present at the death, for some of the information demanded on form B – for instance, whether the deceased had undergone any operation during the final illness or within a year before death; if the deceased had had a pacemaker and whether this has been removed.

Form C, the confirmatory medical certificate, has to be completed by a doctor who has been registered as a medical practitioner in the UK for at least 5 years, who must not be a relative of the deceased nor a relative or partner of the doctor who completed form B. The second doctor also has to see the body before he completes the form.

Each of the doctors is entitled to a fee (minimum fee recommended by the British Medical Association is £18.65 each) for the completion of the certificates, and may also charge travelling expenses. A fee (recommended BMA minimum £27.75) may be charged by a doctor for removing a pacemaker before cremation.

Form C is not required where death occurred in hospital as an inpatient and a post mortem examination has already been carried out by a pathologist of not less than 5 years' standing and the result is known to the doctor completing form B.

Forms B and C are not required when a coroner has issued a certificate for cremation (which is free). When a death is reported to the coroner, you must let him know from the outset if you want the body to be cremated, so that his authority to dispose of it will be in the form of a certificate for cremation (otherwise you may have to go back to him to get the proper certificate). In the rare cases when the coroner has reason for not allowing the body to be cremated, he will not give a certificate for cremation but will issue an order for burial instead. The next of kin must accept this, or wait until he does authorise cremation.

The final authority to cremate the body is given on form F, signed by yet another doctor, the medical referee of the crematorium. He usually does so on the basis of the medical evidence of forms B and C, or after he has received a coroner's certificate for cremation. The medical referee has the power to refuse authority to cremate, and if he cannot be fully satisfied through forms B and C, he may himself order a post mortem or refer the matter to the coroner. The relatives of the deceased have no right to prevent this. If they do not want a post mortem to be held, they will have to forgo cremation and have the body buried instead. If they agree to the post mortem, they will have to pay for it (in rare cases, the crematorium does so). Most crematoria include the fee for the medical referee's services in the total charge for cremation.

If the body of a stillborn child is to be cremated, a special medical certificate has to be completed by a doctor who was present at the stillbirth or who examined the body. No second medical certificate is required. The crematorium's medical referee has to complete form F, giving his authority to cremate.

The purpose of all these forms is to prevent any body being cremated while there are any possible doubts about the circumstances of the death.

crematoria

The majority of crematoria are run by local authorities. Each crematorium has its own scale of fees and there is considerable variation between them. Many crematoria have brochures giving details of what they offer and their charges. Crematoria do not cremate at the weekend; some make an additional or double charge for cremation out of normal working hours.

the service

The charge for a cremation usually includes the fee for the use of the crematorium's chapel, whether you have a service there or not. The chapel is non-denominational. Some crematoria have a roster of chaplains of various denominations. But it is usually expected that arrangements for a clergyman, priest or minister to take a service at the crematorium will be made by the family or undertaker.

If you do not wish it, there is no need to have a religious service at the crematorium, but you should make this clear at the time of booking.

Crematoria work to a strict appointments system, so any service has to be fairly short, unless a special booking is made for a longer period.

Recorded music in the crematorium chapel is usually included in the fee, or there may be an organ.

FOR CREMATION – THE DOCUMENTS

		required before cremation can be applied for	
registrar's certificate for cremation (the disposal certificate)	from registrar	required before cremation can be applied for	via relative and under-taker to crematorium authorities; part C returns to registrar
or after post mortem or inquest: coroner's certificate for cremation	from coroner	authorises disposal of body (supersedes forms B and C)	
form A	from crematorium via undertaker, to be completed by executor or next of kin	applies for cremation and confirms arrangements	to crema-torium authorities
form B†	from crematorium via undertaker, to be completed by deceased's doctor	certifies cause of death	to medical referee at crematorium
form C‡	from crematorium via undertaker, to be completed by a second	confirms cause of death in form B	to medical referee at crematorium

form F	from crematorium, to be completed by medical referee	authorises cremation	kept by crematorium authorities
form —	from crematorium via undertaker, to be completed by executor or next of kin	confirms arrangements; gives instructions for disposal of ashes	to crematorium authorities
certificate for disposal of cremated remains (for burial)	from crematorium	confirms cremation and gives details of the death	via relatives to burial authorities
certificate of cremation	from crematorium	copy of entry in register	to executor or next of kin

† not required if coroner's certificate of cremation
‡ not required after qualifying post mortem

BEFORE THE FUNERAL

In many cases, the member of the funeral director's staff with whom you have the first interview remains in charge for the whole funeral.

the body

One of the first things the undertaker will want to know is where the body is and whether it is to remain there. If he has to send someone to lay out or take away a body in the middle of the night or at the weekend, he will charge extra. If there has been a post mortem, you must get the undertaker to fetch the body from the mortuary.

If the body is to remain in the house rather than await the funeral at the funeral director's premises, he will arrange for it to be laid out if the nurse or any member of the family has not already done so. A nurse refers to laying out as the 'last offices', the undertaker calls it the 'first offices'.

If the undertaker takes the body away without having laid it out, he will want to know what to do with clothing and any jewellery that he takes off the body and will ask what he should dress the body in – shroud or robe, or the deceased's own nightwear.

When he comes to collect a body from the house or a hospital, the undertaker uses either a covered stretcher or a form of coffin which is called a shell. He takes the body away in a small hearse or in an ambulance, or in an anonymous-looking van known in the trade as a handy. In order to remove a body from a hospital, the undertaker usually has to have some written authority, such as the disposal certificate or an authorisation signed by executor or relative.

Most undertakers will keep the body on their premises until the time of the funeral. Usually relatives (and, with their permission, friends) can go to see the body in what is variously called a chapel of rest, reposing room or slumber room. With some undertakers, you have to make an appointment beforehand.

Some undertakers also have their own chapel for private prayer in which a religious service can be held at the beginning of the funeral, before going to the cemetery or crematorium.

embalming

Because it is easier to deal with a body when it has been embalmed, most undertakers like to embalm the body and some insist on doing so. They are likely to call it preservative or hygienic treatment. If you do not want the body to be embalmed, tell the funeral director, because some embalm any body brought to their premises without specifically asking the family about it.

Before a body is embalmed, the doctor must have given his medical certificate of cause of death. It would be unwise to embalm until a disposal certificate has been given by the registrar. If the body is to be cremated, the two doctors must have completed the forms for cremation before the body is embalmed. If the death is reported to the coroner, the body must not be embalmed until he has given his authority.

Embalming, which is intended to delay the process of decomposition, involves replacing blood with a solution of formalin and other chemicals. It is temporary and is not comparable to the ancient egyptian process of mummification. In this country, embalmers tend not to use cosmetics, but try to create an appearance of sleep. An embalmer should be qualified by examination and abide by the code of practice laid down by the British Institute of Embalmers.

A body can be embalmed at home, but usually the embalming is done at the undertaker's.

In a mortuary, the bodies are kept refrigerated, and some undertakers, too, use this method of preservation instead of embalming. When relatives then come to see the body, it is brought from the cold room to the undertaker's chapel or to one of the reposing rooms.

final arrangements

The undertaker must have the registrar's disposal certificate (or the coroner's equivalent authorisation) before confirming the final arrangements. He will see to it that all official forms are completed and taken to the right people at the right time. For a burial, for instance, he takes charge of any grave deeds and gets a cemetery's form of application signed by the executor.

In effect, the funeral director should co-ordinate the various operations at the different stages. He will approach the people in charge of wherever it has been decided the burial or cremation is to take place (this usually means the local clergyman or superintendent of the cemetery or crematorium) in order to reserve a time and, for a burial, to order the type of grave you want.

For a cremation, the undertaker sees that a relative or the executor completes the form of application and the form giving instructions for disposal of the ashes. He will also arrange for two doctors to complete forms B and C and pay them their fees and, when he has gathered the necessary forms, he will get them to the medical referee at the crematorium.

Most crematoria produce at least one other form on which the person organising the funeral confirms any details already provisionally arranged, such as the date and time of cremation. Some crematoria ask for specific instructions about the disposal of the ashes on this form, others have yet another form for this.

The forms have to be submitted to the medical referee of the crematorium by a stipulated time – never less than twenty-four hours – before the cremation is due. The reservation of a time for the cremation is accepted subject to the forms reaching the crematorium within the specified time limit and the fees being paid in advance.

The fees – to vicar, sexton, gravedigger, organist, choirmaster, chaplain and officials at the cemetery or crematorium, as the case may be – usually have to be paid in advance. The funeral director will make the actual payments and will add the charges to his total account.

for the service

The funeral director can be asked to make the arrangements for whatever service is to be held.

There is no obligation to have a service in church, and a service can be held in the churchyard or cemetery. An anglican burial can be taken by the incumbent or, with his permission, by any other clergyman, such as a member of the family or the clergyman whose church the deceased normally attended.

Either the undertaker or a member of the family should ask whoever the family wants to officiate at any service, whether he is willing to do so and whether he will be available at the time planned for holding the ceremony.

If you want a particular piece of music to be played, you should ask for this when making arrangements for the service.

A service in a crematorium or cemetery chapel is restricted by the time allowed – normally half an hour.

igious denominations have some form of funeral ceremony. In this country, unless the dead person had professed another religion, one of the Church of England services will probably be said at his funeral.

Rituals can be adapted according to the preferences of those concerned. For instance, the main part of the service can be said in the church or at the funeral director's with only a few words of committal at the graveside, or all the service can be at the grave. A funeral address may be given either in the church or outside, or not at all.

If you are having an unusual form of service, you can arrange through the funeral director or officiant for special service sheets to be printed.

other denominations

Denominational burial grounds usually insist on their own form of service. If you are involved in arranging the funeral of someone of a faith different from your own, get in touch as soon as possible with the equivalent of the local parish priest of that denomination, to find out what needs to be done.

With orthodox jews, the body should be buried as soon as possible once the disposal certificate is issued. If a man subscribes to a synagogue burial society, he or his wife or his dependent children will be buried, free, by the society in its cemetery. The funeral and coffin will be very simple, and there will be no flowers. Orthodox jews do not get cremated, and embalming or bequeathing a body for medical purposes is not allowed. Reform non-orthodox jews are more flexible, and permit cremation. The funeral will always be simple, but flowers are allowed. A jewish burial society may agree to carry out the funeral of a jew who was not a member of a synagogue and had not been subscribing to any burial society, but his family will be charged for the funeral and the cost will be considerable. There is rarely any difference between the funeral of members of the same synagogue; all are simple. If a jew dies when away from home, it is the responsibility and expense of the relatives to bring the body back for the synagogue burial society to take over.

For a practising roman catholic, it is usual to arrange for the priest to say a requiem mass in the local parish church and for him to take the funeral service. There are no set fees laid down for roman catholic priests to charge for funeral services, but it is usual for the deceased's family to make an offering to the church. Cremation is no longer discouraged for roman catholics, and crematoria have roman catholic priests on their roster.

non-religious service
There is no necessity to have a religious ceremony, or indeed any kind of ceremony at all, at a funeral. However, because some kind of religious ceremony is customary, if you do not want one or the dead person had made it clear that he did not want one, it is important that the executor or whoever is in charge of the arrangements makes this known well before the funeral.

If a body is to be buried in a churchyard without a religious ceremony, or with a ceremony held by an officiant of another denomination, you should give the incumbent of the parish 48 hours' notice in writing; in practice, it should be possible to make the necessary arrangements in a telephone conversation. The usual parish regulations and fees still apply.

If a body is to be buried in a cemetery or cremated at a crematorium without a religious ceremony, tell the undertaker or the authorities at the time the funeral is being arranged. There will normally be no difficulties, provided it is clear that the proceedings will be properly conducted.

Where there is not going to be a religious ceremony, whoever is in charge of the funeral arrangements must also make arrangements for the details of the ceremony.

If you want no ceremony at all, the usual procedure is for a few members of the family or close friends to attend the committal in silence or with some music being played. If you want a non-religious ceremony without an officiant, on the lines of a Friends' meeting, you must make sure that those present either know already how such a ceremony works or are told at the beginning.

The more usual procedure is to have an officiant who prepares and conducts the ceremony, on the lines of a minister. This may be a member of the family or a close friend, or a representative of an appropriate organisation or a sympathetic religious minister. The only qualification is some experience of handling meetings. Business, professional and labour organisations generally contain such people, and so do humanist societies.

The national freethought organisations in London all give help with funerals: they can offer information and advice by telephone or post, or send literature, or sometimes provide officiants. Try the British Humanist Association, 13 Prince of Wales Terrace, London W8 5PG; the National Secular Society, 702 Holloway Road, London N19 3NL; the Rationalist Press Association, 88 Islington High Street, London N1 8EW; the South Place Ethical Society, Conway Hall, 25 Red Lion Square, London WC1R 4RL.

In the West Midlands region, there is a network of humanist funeral officiators who can be contacted through the Coventry officiator (14 Coundon Road, Coventry CV1 4AW; telephone 0203 20070) or the Birmingham officiator (96 Wentworth Road, Birmingham B17 9SY; telephone 021-427 8995). For the southern counties of England, the number to contact is 0273 556744.

The British Humanist Association charges £2 for its book-let *Humanist Funeral Ceremonies*, and the other organisations appreciate donations for their material. Their officiants would expect to be paid a fee and expenses, probably costing more than for a religious minister because of the amount of preparation and travelling involved.

A non-religious ceremony may take any form, provided it is decent and orderly. The usual procedure is for the officiant to explain the ceremony, after which there may be readings of appropriate prose or poetry, tributes either by the officiant or by others present, and the playing of appro-priate music; it is common to allow moments of silence in which religious people present may add their prayers to the occasion.

Such non-religious ceremonies are designed not in oppo-sition to religious ceremonies but as alternatives for people who would prefer not to have the customary service or would feel it hyprocritical to have one, but may not be aware that anything else is possible.

notices

Announcements of deaths are usually made in the national and local newspapers most likely to be read by the deceased's friends and acquaintances. Many newspapers, including the national dailies, will accept the text by tele-phone, provided the office can telephone back to read over to a member of the family or the funeral director the text that is going to be printed. The papers do not usually ask for evidence that the death has occurred, unless the notice is submitted by someone who is not a relative or executor or the funeral director.

When the funeral director inserts the notice on behalf of his client, he may ask if he should include his firm's name and address, usually as being able to supply more information about the funeral or to receive flowers beforehand. The cost of an announcement will be based on the number of lines the notice comes to.

The national daily newspapers insist on a standard form of announcement: the family name of the dead person, the date of death and the place, the deceased's full name (but the papers exercise their editorial control strictly, even to the extent of excising nicknames), home address and often some mention of the remaining family, and of the cause of death.

Details of time, date and place of the funeral can be included. Anyone who has not been specifically invited but wishing to attend is expected to arrive independently at the time and place announced in the press. If the family wants to restrict attendance at the funeral, the notice should say 'funeral private'. When a funeral is announced as private, only those whom the family has asked to come should attend. If the relatives think that a great many people might wish to come, they may arrange for the funeral to be private followed by a memorial service some days or weeks later for all those who wish to pay tribute to the dead person. If no details of the time and place of the funeral are published at all, it is to be assumed that the funeral is to be a private one.

flowers
The notice in the newspaper should also make it clear if no flowers are wanted (or no letters). Sometimes only flowers from the family, or only certain types of flowers are requested.

A 'no flowers' request should be strictly observed. Sometimes other ways are suggested in which sympathy can be expressed: for example, by giving plants or shrubs to the cemetery or crematorium garden. The more usual alternative is to suggest in the newspaper notice that donations be made in the name of the deceased to a particular charity or organisation in which he or she was interested.

For flowers, the newspaper notice should specifically state where they are to be sent. If the flowers go direct to the cemetery or crematorium or to the undertaker's, the undertaker can be asked to make a list of the people who have sent flowers, so that the next of kin have a record afterwards. He will transport the flowers with the coffin to the church, cemetery or crematorium.

When the body is buried, the flowers are left on or near the grave. A crematorium may restrict where flowers can be put and reserve the right to dispose of flowers afterwards.

THE FUNERAL

You can arrange with the funeral director that the funeral shall start from your home or from his premises, usually depending on where the body is. Or you can ask him to take the body direct to the church, cemetery or crematorium for mourners to meet there. If the undertaker provides cars for the family and other special mourners, he will marshal the cortege and arrange when it shall start. Timing is important because the cemetery or crematorium authorities work to a very tight timetable and you may be penalised if the funeral is late.

Burglars have been known to select victims by reading funeral announcements in the newspapers and breaking into the unoccupied house during the funeral. So, try to arrange for someone to be in or to keep an eye on the house while you are at the funeral.

You should discuss and make a clear arrangement with the funeral director beforehand about the procedure at the end of the funeral – for instance, whether you want him to take people home – and at what point you will not need him any more. Tell the undertaker not to incur extra expenses without your authorisation – in case funeral guests ask him to drive them to the railway station twelve miles away, or the clergyman requests to be picked up or taken home by car.

Before the undertaker closes the lid of the coffin, he may ask the relatives or executors if they would like to witness this and see the body again (euphemistically, to pay their last respects). This also acts as a safeguard to check the identity of the body before finally closing the coffin.

burial

At a burial preceded by a church service, the coffin is taken into the church by the bearers and placed in front of the altar. The mourners normally follow the coffin. In some anglican as well as roman catholic churches, the coffin may be taken into the church the previous evening, and remains there before the altar until the service.

After the service, the bearers take the coffin from the church to the grave while the mourners follow, led there by a member of the graveyard or cemetery staff. If the service has been held elsewhere, or there is no service, the coffin is carried direct from the hearse to the grave.

At some more formal funerals, there are pall bearers who walk alongside the coffin but do not carry anything. Originally, they used to carry the pall, a heavy canopy which was held over the coffin.

The bearers lower the coffin into the grave, on webbing slings, while the words of committal are said. The mourners sometimes throw earth on to the coffin, but they usually do not stay to see the complete filling-in of the grave, which is done later by the cemetery or graveyard staff.

A register of burials in the parish is kept by the church, and every cemetery has to keep a register of burials and a record of who owns a grave plot and who has already been buried in each grave. Copies of entries in the register can be bought at any time for a small fee.

The family of anyone who is buried in a churchyard is responsible for looking after the grave. The parochial church council is responsible for looking after the churchyard generally and keeping the paths and walks and unused parts tidy. When granting a faculty, some diocese stipulate that a contribution be made towards the upkeep of the churchyard.

cremation

Before a cremation, either the service takes place in a church with the words of committal said at the crematorium chapel, or the whole service is held at the crematorium. The coffin is taken into the crematorium chapel, followed by the mourners, and placed on the catafalque.

As the committal sentences are being said, the coffin passes out of sight, by being lowered or moved mechanically through a door, or by a curtain being drawn across it. You may be given an option for this not to happen until everyone has left the chapel, and in some crematoria there is no provision for removing the coffin during the service so that the mourners leave while the coffin is still in the chapel.

The coffin goes into the committal room, to await cremation. If no religious service is being held, the coffin may pass straight into the committal room. The body is not taken out of the coffin, and each coffin is burnt individually in a cremator (which is what the special type of furnace is called).

When making arrangements for the cremation, the executors or next of kin can ask to be allowed to go into the committal room to see the coffin placed in the cremator. Usually only two people are allowed.

Each crematorium has to keep a register of its cremations. You can get a certified copy of an entry in the register, for which a small charge is made. You are only likely to need such evidence if for some reason the death has not been registered in this country, or ashes are being sent to another country which has stringent requirements about the identity of a parcel containing cremated remains.

the ashes

If a relative wants to take away the cremated remains, they can be collected from the crematorium about 24 hours after the cremation, in a container provided by the crematorium.

For a charge (plus postage), the crematorium will post the ashes to the person who applied for the cremation. Because the ashes are in the form of very fine powder, they are usually sealed in a polythene bag inside the container, to prevent any escaping.

The undertaker may be willing to collect the ashes and post or give them to you, or keep the ashes until they are to be disposed of. Most undertakers offer a selection of urns or special boxes for you to put the ashes in. Some undertakers will, for a fee, keep ashes until the time when they can be mingled with the ashes of, say, the widower or widow, to be scattered or buried together.

Arrangements such as these do not need to be made at the funeral. You can see the funeral director later.

The person taking away the ashes from the crematorium usually has to sign a receipt for them and may be asked to state how they will be finally disposed of.

With the ashes, the crematorium gives or sends a certificate which confirms that the cremation has taken place. This certificate, which is usually free, will be required by the church or cemetery authorities where the ashes are going to be buried or scattered.

The crematorium will keep ashes free of charge for a limited time, usually a month. Then, in the absence of any special instructions, after giving 14 days' notice, the ashes are either buried or scattered, whichever is the practice at the particular crematorium. The basic fee in many crematoria includes scattering or burial; otherwise this costs anything up to £10 extra. A crematorium charges an additional fee for scattering ashes from a cremation elsewhere. If you want the crematorium to keep ashes for a period longer than the time it normally keeps them without charge, you will have to pay on a monthly basis.

disposal of the ashes

There is no law regulating the disposal of cremated remains.

Ashes can be scattered, anywhere, provided it is not done too flamboyantly or carelessly.

The undertaker will, for a fee, scatter the ashes for you in a suitable part of a park or garden.

A crematorium scatters or buries ashes in what it calls its garden of remembrance. The ground there is usually not consecrated and the place is not marked. The deceased's family can ask to witness the proceedings (some crematoria charge a fee), but there is generally no formal ceremony.

The Church of England has certain stipulations about the disposal of ashes in consecrated ground: scattering is discouraged and direct committal into the earth is preferred, by burial or by strewing (lifting a portion of turf, spreading the ashes on the earth and replacing the turf).

Ashes can be buried in most churchyards and cemeteries. Some have a separate section for this.

Burying ashes in a churchyard of cemetery can be done with as much or as little ceremony as the relatives wish, by arrangement with the incumbent of the parish or with the superintendent of the cemetery. The interment fee for burying ashes in a churchyard is the same as that for a body; in a cemetery, less. Burial of ashes is sometimes permitted in a churchyard which has had to be closed for ordinary burials, but a faculty may be required.

You may be allowed to set a small plaque into the ground or nearby wall to mark the place in the churchyard where the ashes were put. Some churches keep a book of remembrance inside the church; a charge of a few pounds is made for an entry in this.

AFTER THE FUNERAL

Afterwards, light refreshments may be provided for the mourners, usually in the house of a member of the immediate family, or at a local restaurant. Make sure that mourners are told if this has been arranged and where they are to go.

paying for the funeral
The funeral director will send in his account fairly soon after the funeral. He is likely to offer a discount for full payment within a stipulated time – say, two or four weeks. The funeral director will, however, understand if you tell him that the bill cannot be paid until a grant of probate or letters of administration have been issued.

The funeral director's account should be as detailed as possible, and show separately what is due to him for his services and the coffin, and what he has paid out on your behalf (where possible, with receipted bills): the burial or cremation charges, doctors' fees, and any other payments he made, such as the cost of any flowers you asked him to order. This will enable you to check that no tips or other extras were paid out except those you had specifically requested him to give. Tips to bearers, grave diggers, cemetery or crematorium staff could mount up considerably.

Many of the payments that the funeral director will have made for you are expenses you would have incurred anyway. He may have inserted a notice in the newspaper on your behalf, or arranged catering for the funeral, or ordered special stationery.

The funeral director's charges for the funeral, including the supply of a coffin and the carriage, are exempt from value added tax, and so is the fee for burial or cremation, and any fee paid to a clergyman for conducting the funeral service.

For any goods or services concerned with the commemoration of the dead – for example, a headstone, plant, entry in a book of remembrance – value added tax has to be paid.

memorials

A headstone or other monument or memorial in a churchyard or cemetery is subject to the restrictions imposed by the church or by the cemetery. There will be stipulations affecting the size, shape and material of any memorial and the words and lettering of an inscription. Many burial grounds and nearly all churchyards nowadays prohibit kerbs or surrounds to graves, and memorials are usually restricted to a headstone or a plinth and vase set at the head of the grave.

Neither reserving a grave in a churchyard by faculty nor paying a burial fee gives you the right to put up a monument or other embellishment on the grave. For this, approval must be given by the incumbent and a further fee paid. The Parochial Fees Order lays down the fees for permission to put up a monument with an inscription or to add an inscription to an existing monument. The fees proposed from 1 January 1987 are

small cross of wood	£3.50
small vase	£10.00
small tablet commemorating cremated remains	£17.50
inscription added to existing monument	£9.50
any other monument	£41.50
(such as headstone, flatstone, cross, larger vase)	

Anything other than a simple tombstone or inscription requires a faculty.

When permission is given to erect a monument or memorial over a non-faculty grave, this does not confer exclusive use of the grave.

The wording of an inscription must be approved in writing by the incumbent; most will object to colloquialism and informal descriptions, and generally stipulate that any quotations are biblical or otherwise religious.

The funeral director is not usually involved in these arrangements but he should warn you of any restrictions he knows about memorials when you are choosing between burial grounds. Some funeral directors run a firm of monumental masons in addition to their undertaking business.

arranging for a memorial

When the family or the monumental mason apply to the church or cemetery authorities for permission to do anything to mark the grave, a copy of the entry in the burial register may be asked for. If the grave is a private or faculty one, whoever is applying has to produce the deeds as authorisation and as a means of identifying the grave.

Normally, a headstone cannot be erected, or replaced after a second burial, until the ground has settled over the grave, usually several months after the burial. Less reputable monumental masons, on finding out when a funeral is being held, importune the family with discreditable haste, even at the graveside or by calling at the house on the day of the funeral. Do not yield to their persistence and persuasiveness.

To get the names of established local firms of monumental masons, you can write to the National Association of Master Masons (Crown Buildings, High Street, Aylesbury, Bucks HP20 1SL) for a list of their members in the locality.

You should not commission a monumental mason to carry out any work for you without knowing what the burial ground's regulations are. The mason should be able to advise you on these, and show you in his brochure or display area the various types of memorial that would be suitable. The cost depends on the material – stone, marble, granite – and the size, ornamentation and finish.

Before ordering a memorial, ask for a written estimate clearly stating the items and total cost, including any delivery or erection charges. Value added tax is charged on the cost of adding an inscription to an existing stone and on a new headstone, but not on the removal and replacement of an existing memorial. It is usual for masons to ask for a 10 per cent deposit to be paid by the client when confirming the order for a memorial.

The fee paid to the church or cemetery authorities for permission to erect a memorial is usually paid by the mason and charged to the client on the final account. This fee is exempt from value added tax.

after cremation

About a week after the cremation, the crematorium will probably send a brochure telling you what memorials are offered, with prices (value added tax is chargeable on these). These memorials are optional extras – there is no need to have any of them.

Hand-lettered inscriptions in the book of remembrance, which is kept at the crematorium, usually consist of the name, date of death and a short epitaph. The charge depends on the length of the entry. The crematorium displays the book open at the right page on the anniversary of the death, not of the date of cremation. Some crematoria sell a miniature reproduction of the entry in the book of remembrance, in the form of a card or bound as a booklet. The price of the booklet depends mainly on the luxury of the binding.

The charges for the erection of memorial plaques or for

inscriptions on panels in cloisters or memorial halls vary between crematoria. A number of local authority crematoria, however, allow no memorials other than an entry in the book of remembrance.

In some crematoria, there is a cloister or colonnade, called a columbarium, full of niches. The ashes are either walled in by a plaque or left in an urn in the niche. The charge of renting or buying a niche is high, and in some of the columbaria there are no more spaces left.

Some crematoria allow trees, or more usually rosebushes, to be planted near the spot where ashes are buried or scattered, or allow plaques or memorial seats to be put in the gardens. Again, costs vary, as does the length of time for which the crematorium will see to the maintenance.

CHARTS

of what to do when someone dies

CHART 1

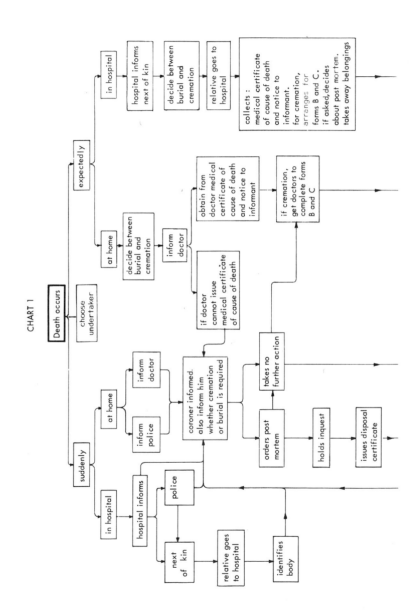

Death occurs

choose undertaker

expectedly

in hospital — hospital informs next of kin — decide between burial and cremation — relative goes to hospital — collects: medical certificate of cause of death and notice to informant. for cremation, arranges for forms B and C. if asked, decides about post mortem. takes away belongings

at home — decide between burial and cremation — inform doctor — obtain from doctor medical certificate of cause of death and notice to informant — if cremation, get doctors to complete forms B and C

if doctor cannot issue medical certificate of cause of death

suddenly

at home — inform doctor / inform police — coroner informed. also inform him whether cremation or burial is required

in hospital — hospital informs — police / next of kin — relative goes to hospital — identifies body

takes no further action

orders post mortem — holds inquest — issues disposal certificate

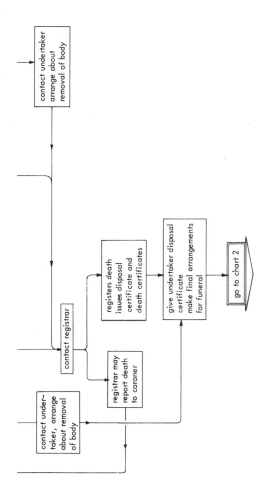

contact undertaker arrange about removal of body

contact registrar

contact undertaker, arrange about removal of body

registrar may report death to coroner

registers death issues disposal certificate and death certificates

give undertaker disposal certificate make final arrangements for funeral

go to chart 2

92

CHART 2

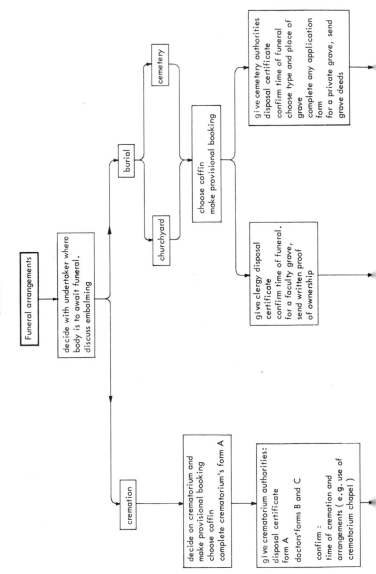

Funeral arrangements

decide with undertaker where body is to await funeral. discuss embalming

cremation

decide on crematorium and make provisional booking
choose coffin
complete crematorium's form A

give crematorium authorities:
disposal certificate
form A
doctors' forms B and C

confirm :
time of cremation and arrangements (e.g. use of crematorium chapel)

burial

churchyard

cemetery

choose coffin
make provisional booking

give clergy disposal certificate
confirm time of funeral.
for a faculty grave, send written proof of ownership

give cemetery authorities
disposal certificate
confirm time of funeral
choose type and place of grave
complete any application form
for a private grave, send grave deeds

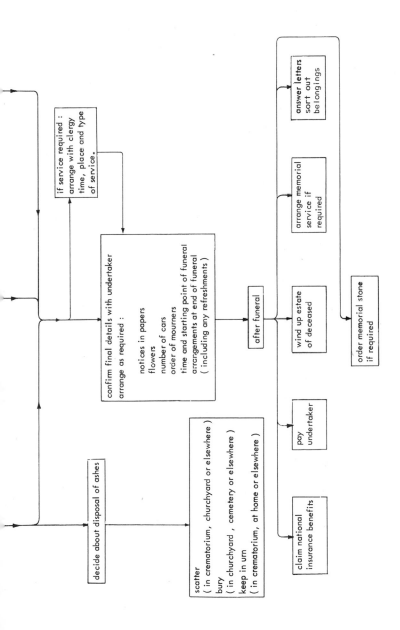

decide about disposal of ashes

if service required :
arrange with clergy
time, place and type
of service.

confirm final details with undertaker
arrange as required :

notices in papers
flowers
number of cars
order of mourners
time and starting point of funeral
arrangements at end of funeral
(including any refreshments)

scatter
(in crematorium, churchyard or elsewhere)
bury
(in churchyard , cemetery or elsewhere)
keep in urn
(in crematorium, at home or elsewhere)

after funeral

claim national
insurance benefits

pay
undertaker

wind up estate
of deceased

arrange memorial
service if
required

answer letters
sort out
belongings

order memorial stone
if required

AWAY FROM HOME

Some people express a wish to be buried near their family although they now live somewhere else. If this is so, or if someone dies in an area other than where he lived, funeral arrangements have to be made in two places. One undertaker will probably cope. If it is too far for him to supervise both ends himself, he may subcontract arrangements at the other end to a colleague, but his contract with the other undertaker is not your concern. Alternatively, you can contact an undertaker in the district to which the body is to be taken and deal with him direct.

A body is sent by road in a hearse whenever possible because this is likely to be a quicker and cheaper means of transport. For long distances, it may be better to send it by air or rail, but you then have to pay for a hearse at both ends of the journey. Charges vary according to the distance or route, but are generally high. An airline may charge double or more the ordinary cargo rate or a special flat rate for carrying a coffin with a body. With the body must be sent the disposal certificate and other documents such as grave deeds. It is usual to embalm the body before sending it on its journey.

sending a body abroad

No official notice has to be given or permission sought when cremated remains are being taken out of this country. Restrictions may, however, be imposed by the authorities of the receiving country. These may be dealt with in this country, normally by permission from the relevant embassy or consulate, who may examine the urn and then seal it.

If the body of someone who has died in England or Wales is going to be buried or cremated in another country (including Scotland, Northern Ireland and the Channel Islands), the coroner of the district in which the body is lying must be told. Form 104 gives 'notice to a coroner of intention to remove a body out of England'. You can get this from the registrar when registering the death, and ask him for the name and address of the coroner to whom it should be sent. If he knows in time that the body is going out of the country, the registrar will not issue a certificate for burial or cremation. If, however, such a certificate has already been given, it must be sent to the coroner when sending him form 104.

If the coroner is already in the process of investigating the death, he will not be able to release the body until it is certain that the body will not be needed for any further examination. He will do this as soon as the circumstances permit.

In other cases, the coroner may sign the form acknowledging the notice of removal, permitting the body to be removed in 4 days' time. This allows time for the coroner to check whether he needs to investigate the death.

If, however, the family need to remove the body quickly for personal reasons or perhaps to take advantage of an available flight, the coroner can sign the form to allow the body to be removed immediately, provided he has been given all the information and documents needed concerning the death. Taking a body out of the jurisdiction removes any evidence as effectively as cremation does, and the restrictions are just as stringent.

making the arrangements
A funeral director will make the arrangements about moving the body by rail, any freight-carrying airline or any shipping line. Transporting a body is expensive. Some airlines charge twice the normal cargo rate for a body in a

coffin. There may be special requirements: for example, that the coffin is enclosed in a crate or that it is airtight. Most airlines insist on the body being embalmed. This requires specially thorough embalming, and a certificate of embalming must accompany the body.

Also, the necessary freight documents must be completed. The consular office of the country to which the body is going will know what regulations have to be met. You will need one standard form of death certificate for the UK customs, and another one, or more, depending on the requirements of the country to which the body is going. You may have to have all documents translated and authenticated at the consulate of the country concerned, for which you will have to pay. The consulate will also tell you what formalities will be required on arrival of the body and what arrangements you can make beforehand.

burial at sea
Burying a body in the sea counts as removal out of England or Wales, and the coroner must be informed accordingly and his acknowledgment of the notice of intended removal obtained.

Permission has to be obtained from the local district inspector of fisheries (addresses available from the Fisheries Inspectorate, MAFF, Great Westminster House, Horseferry Road, London SW1P 2AE). Permission may not be granted along certain stretches of the coast.

The fisheries inspector should be able to suggest a suitable ship whose master knows the local tides and coast and will advise on a position least likely to yield up the body once it has been committed. The cost is a matter of bargaining between you and the master of the vessel from which the body is to be lowered. If a coffin is used, it needs to be weighted and have holes bored in it to make sure that it sinks.

If the body has been cremated, the ashes can be scattered on to the sea anywhere, from a boat or the beach. This operation also requires permission from the local district inspector of fisheries. An urn with ashes should preferably not be deposited in the sea; if this is unavoidable, the urn should be pierced to enable it to sink more quickly.

death abroad

When a british subject dies abroad, whether as a resident there or as a visitor, his death must be registered according to local requirements and regulations. The british consul in that country can also register the death. The advantage of the death being registered by a british consul is that certified copies of the entry of death can eventually be obtained from the General Register Office in London, just as if the death had been registered here in the normal way. Otherwise there is no official record in this country of the death.

When someone dies on a foreign ship or aircraft, it counts as a death abroad. On a british-registered ship or aircraft, the death is recorded in the captain's log for the day. Eventually, a copy of the log entry can be obtained from the General Register Office in London.

bringing a body from abroad

If you want to get back to this country the body of a person who died abroad, you can ask the british consul there, or the Foreign Office consular department in London, about the formalities and procedure (but they cannot provide financial assistance).

Some of the larger firms of funeral directors have agents abroad and can arrange either to have a funeral in the other country or to bring the body back here. Bringing a body back is likely to cost several hundred pounds, or even thousands.

When the body is brought back, the UK customs require some evidence of the death to come with the body, such as a death certificate issued in the place where death occurred, or some official authorisation to remove the body issued by a local coroner (or equivalent).

The death does not have to be registered in England or Wales but you will need from the registrar for the district where the body is to be buried or cremated, a certificate of no liability to register, which is the equivalent of the green disposal certificate.

Whoever is arranging the funeral must supply the registrar with evidence that the death took place outside England or Wales. This evidence is a death certificate issued by the civil registrar of the place where death occurred or an official authorisation to remove the body or, if the death took place in Scotland or Northern Ireland, a death certificate issued there.

If a body brought from outside the UK is to be cremated, a doctor's statement of the medical cause of death must be sent with it (this may have to be translated and authenticated). You or the undertaker should send or take the completed cremation application form A and all the documents which came with the body to the Home Office, E4 division, 50 Queen Anne's Gate, London SW1H 9AT. It is wise to telephone beforehand to check that you have all the necessary documents: the telephone number is 01-213 7006 or 3044. If you post them, put 'cremation urgent ' on the envelope. Provided the death was from a specific natural cause, the Home Office then issues a certificate to take the place of forms B and C for the crematorium's medical referee.

There is a problem with certain countries, particularly France, where domestic law prohibits the doctor certifying death to be more specific than 'natural causes' (where appropriate). This is insufficient in the UK where a precise cause is required. It is often possible for the local british consul to obtain the precise cause of death by a personal approach to the doctor there, but where this fails, it is necessary for the case to be passed to the coroner.

In any case where the coroner assumes jurisdiction, his authority is overriding and the Home Office will not intervene.

In most cases, the coroner in whose area the body is first received into the country must be informed. The funeral director arranging the funeral normally does this. The coroner then decides whether to accept the paperwork that comes with the body or to order further inquiries. He may order a post mortem, and in the case of unnatural death he will hold an inquest. The results of this may, however, be inconclusive because the body may have been embalmed or decomposed, or witnesses cannot be summoned, and there is no obligation on another country to provide any information or to cooperate in any inquiry.

In a case of natural death, the coroner will issue his certificate for cremation so that cremation can go ahead; if it is to be a burial, he will issue a certificate of no liability to register, to be taken to the registrar in whose district the burial is to take place, for him to issue a disposal certificate to authorise the burial.

REMOVAL TO OR FROM OTHER COUNTRIES
THE DOCUMENTS

form 104 (notice to a coroner of intention to move a body out of England)		from registrar, to be completed by executor or next of kin	gives notice that body will be taken out of country	to coroner of place where body is
coroner's form acknowledging removal notice		from coroner	confirms that body may be removed after four days	to executor or next of kin, to send with body
if death abroad: certificate of no liability to register		from registrar or coroner		
	part A	to be completed by relative	declares details of death and applies for part B	to registrar
	part B	to be completed by registrar	states that death is not required to be registered; takes place of disposal certificate	to person who completed part A
	part C	to be completed by church, cemetery or crematorium	confirms that burial or cremation has taken place	to registrar who issued part B

death when in armed forces

If a member of the forces dies serving abroad, the Ministry of Defence normally allows the next of kin the following choices

○ a funeral overseas with two people from the UK (normally the next of kin) attending, all at public expense
○ repatriation of the body at public expense to an undertaker in the UK chosen by the family. Once the body has reached the undertaker, the family become responsible for the funeral. The Ministry of Defence provides the coffin and a grant of £220 to assist with the funeral expenses.

If a serviceman dies in this country, his next of kin can choose to have

○ a funeral at public expense
This will be arranged and paid for by the Ministry of Defence, provided that it takes place near to where the death occurred. (Exceptionally, because military funerals cannot be arranged in Northern Ireland, servicemen dying there can be buried anywhere in the UK at public expense.)
○ a private funeral with limited military assistance
The Ministry of Defence pays for the coffin and the conveyance of the body some distance from the place of death to an undertaker chosen by the family. Once the body has reached the undertaker, the family are responsible for the funeral. The Ministry of Defence pays a grant of £220 to assist with the funeral costs.
○ a private expense funeral
The next of kin claim the body and make all the arrangements privately (including the provision of a coffin). In this case, the Ministry of Defence allows a grant of £355.

A member of the forces who dies while serving may be buried in a military cemetery by consultation with the appropriate cemetery authorities. This will only be arranged at public expense if there is a military cemetery near to where the death occurred.

If someone who was receiving a war disablement pension dies as a result of that disablement or was drawing a constant attendance allowance, the Department of Health and Social Security may arrange and pay for a simple funeral. The next of kin should contact the local war pensioners' welfare office straightaway, before any formal arrangements are made.

SCOTLAND

The certificate of registration of death which the registrar has given to the informant must be given to the person in charge of the place of interment or cremation. No part of the certificate is returned to the registrar.

burial

In Scotland, a grave is referred to as a lair. As in England, it is possible to purchase the exclusive right of burial in a cemetery or kirkyard plot, either in perpetuity or for a limited period. Most kirkyards are administered by the social work department of the local authority. In Scotland, cemetery chapels are rare.

At a burial, silk tassselled cords, called courtesy cords, are attached to the coffin. Specific mourners are sent a card beforehand inviting them to hold a cord while the coffin bearers take the strain of the lowering. Courtesy cords are not used for the burial of cremated remains.

A pad or mattress is often put on top of the coffin as a development of the old custom of putting grass or straw over the coffin to muffle the sound of the earth falling on the lid when the grave is filled in.

cremation

The regulations and procedure for cremation are the same as in England and Wales since the Cremation Regulations 1965 brought these into line with those of Scotland.

sending a body abroad

There are no formalities connected with the removal of bodies out of Scotland for either cremation or burial in another country, but you should ensure that the death has been registered in Scotland before moving the body out of Scotland. The procurator fiscal does not have to be informed.

If the body is being taken to England or Wales for burial, the certificate of registration (form 14) or the standard death certificate must be produced to the registrar there.

No formal notice has to be given or permission sought when cremated remains are being taken out of the country.

bringing a body from abroad

There is no need to produce evidence for the registrar in Scotland that the death took place elsewhere. If the body is coming from England or Wales, the person in charge of the place of interment or cremation in Scotland will require the coroner's form permitting the body to be removed.

When a body is brought into Scotland to be cremated there, the authority of the Secretary of State for Scotland must be obtained before cremation can be carried out. This means applying to the Scottish Home and Health Department, St Andrew's House, Edinburgh EH1 3DE, with any supporting papers such as a foreign death certificate.

Cremated remains brought into Scotland must be accompanied by a certificate of cremation issued by the crematorium.

WHAT ELSE HAS TO BE DONE

None of the deceased's property should be sold nor, strictly speaking, given away until probate has been granted, or letters of administration issued. In the course of getting probate (if the person who died left a will) or letters of administration (if he died intestate), the deceased's personal representative must inform the bank, who will stop payment of all cheques and banker's orders; notify the post office, building society or any other institution where the deceased had an account, who will temporarily freeze any savings held there; and notify the tax inspector. After the grant of probate or letters of administration, the personal representative settles the debts, obtains payment of any life insurance policy, and transfers the ownership of any house, shares or other property the deceased may have had. A detailed account of how to administer an estate is given in the Consumer Publication *Wills and probate*.

pensions and tax

All pension books and allowance books of the deceased must be returned either to the issuing office quoted in the book or to the Department of Health and Social Security (keep a note of the pension or allowance number). If there are any uncashed orders which are due, they must not be cashed after the death, even if they have already been signed. Any unpaid amounts should be claimed when the book is returned. Unless the executors or next of kin make a specific claim, no repayments are offered by the DHSS for any outstanding pensions or allowances.

To get any unpaid portions of a war pension, write to the Department of Health and Social Security, War Pensions Issue Office, Norcross, Blackpool FY5 3TA, and claim the amount due, quoting the pension number.

If the deceased had been an officer in one of the armed forces and a pension or allowance was being paid on the basis of his war service, the next payment that comes will have to be returned, uncashed, to the issuing office. Send with it a note of the place and date of death, and claim any amount that has become due in the period from the last payment to the death.

If income tax was being deducted from the dead person's salary under the pay-as-you-earn scheme, a refund of tax may be due, depending on the date of death and the tax paid up to then. You will have to apply to the inspector of taxes for the area where the deceased's tax affairs were dealt with; if no one contacts him about a refund, he will not do anything about it. (The executors will hear from the collector of taxes if there is any tax to be paid.)

A widow gets a bereavement allowance in the form of the married man's full tax allowance set against her income for the tax year in which her husband died and for the following tax year.

The Inland Revenue leaflet IR45 *What happens when someone dies* gives a brief outline of tax matters after a death.

home and possessions
Responsibility may need to be transferred into the name of another person for a house or flat. Relatives who were living with the deceased in rented accommodation should seek advice about their rights, from their citizens advice bureau or a solicitor. (The landlord is not likely to be the best person to advise, because he may be motivated by his own interests.)

The Consumer Publication *Renting and letting* includes information on the rights of successors to remain in rented property, whether private or council, even if the tenancy was in the name of the deceased person.

Depending on her income and circumstances, a widow (like anyone else) may be eligible for housing benefit paid through the local authority to help with the rates (and the basic rent, if a tenant). Explanatory booklets (£1 each) for home owners, council and private tenants are available from SHAC (189a Old Brompton Road, London SW5 0AR).

If the telephone was in the dead person's name, the executor or next of kin should write to the area telephone manager to tell him of the death and ask for the telephone account up to the date of death so that it can be paid out of the estate.

Where appropriate, the executor should also write to the local electricity board and gas region to cancel the deceased's contract and to ask for the meter to be read so that the debt can be met from the estate. The relevant authority should be told who will now be responsible for the account.

If the dead person had been getting meals-on-wheels or a home help, tell the local authority social services department that this service is no longer required, and return any aid or appliance that was on loan.

Any library books or records should be taken back to avoid getting a series of reminders and possibly a fine.

If relatives have to arrange to clear a flat or house quickly, furniture which is not required can be offered to a local dealer or auctioneer, and anything which is not saleable will sometimes be accepted by local charities. If you have to arrange with the local authority refuse department for a special collection, a charge may be made.

Sometimes following the announcement of a death in the papers, secondhand clothes dealers call round at the house and offer to buy the dead person's clothes. This is a simple way of getting rid of the clothes if you want to, although you will probably not be offered much for them. Remember to look through pockets and handbags before letting the clothes go. If you want to give the clothes to a charity, you will almost certainly have to pay the cost of getting them there. Some auctioneers have occasional sales of clothing. You have to get the clothes to the auction rooms and the auctioneer will send you the money paid for the clothes, minus his commission, a little while after the auction. Alternatively, you can offer the clothes for sale, singly or as a complete wardrobe, through a local advertisement or good-as-new shop.

Other unwanted possessions of a dead person, such as books, cameras, sports equipment, can be sold by being advertised or offered to a local dealer or secondhand shop, or can be given to a charity.

In some localities, there are house clearance dealers who undertake to remove everything for a lump sum. You should make it part of the arrangement that the house is left completely empty, and clean.

bits of paper
When going through the dead person's belongings, you will probably find various tickets and documents.

The deceased's medical card should be sent to the registrar of deaths if it was not taken at the time of registering the death.

A rail season ticket should be taken to the station where it was issued and a refund claimed. The station may require to see proof of probate or letters of administration. If the ticket had not been used recently, either because the deceased had been ill for a long time before his death or because the ticket was not discovered until some time afterwards, before backdating the refund the station will require evidence, such as a death certificate or doctor's certificate. No refund is given for surrendered railcards.

A London underground/bus season ticket may be surrendered at any underground station or may be posted (recorded delivery advisable) to the commercial office of London Regional Transport, 55 Broadway, London SW1H 0BD. The refund will be made from the last day of use if a medical or death certificate is produced, otherwise from the date of surrender. The refund is made payable to the widow or widower without formality; alternatively, to the executor on production of proof of probate or letters of administration, or a letter from a solicitor authorising payment to that person.

You should send a passport back with a letter of explanation to the Passport Office, Clive House, 70 Petty France, London SW1H 9HD, or to the passport office in Liverpool, Newport (Gwent), Peterborough, Glasgow, Belfast. You can ask to have it back, if you wish, after cancellation.

If the deceased owned a car, once the new ownership of the car has been settled, the top half of the registration document should be given to the new owner/keeper and the other half sent to the Driving and Vehicle Licensing Centre, Swansea SA99 1AR, so that the change can be recorded and a new document issued. The insurance for the car should be altered straightaway.

For all other insurance policies in the deceased's name, the insurance companies should be notified, and asked to cancel the policies and to refund any unexpired premiums, or to amend the policy to another name.

claiming money due
Clubs and associations to which the dead person belonged should be told of his death and any unwanted subscriptions

cancelled. There may be a refund to claim on unexpired memberships.

To claim on a life insurance policy, send the policy to the company together with the standard death certificate. A policy made 'in trust' for the widow/widower or other named beneficiary bypasses probate, and payment can be made to the beneficiary straightaway. In all other cases, payment may be delayed until probate is granted. If this is longer than two months after the date of death, the insurance company must add interest, at the current market rate, from then until the payment is made.

A number of employers have a life insurance scheme that pays out a lump sum on the death of an employee. And most company pension schemes provide either a cash sum or a pension (sometimes both) for dependants. Find out from the dead person's last employers whether any such payments are now due.

Various societies, professional bodies, trade unions and ex-service organisations run benevolent schemes for the dependants of their members or of people who qualify within the scope of the organisation. A widow should get in touch with the secretary of any organisation related to her late husband's activities to find out what benevolent schemes might be available.

personal support

Cruse, the national organisation for widows, widowers and their children, offers help through counselling for the individual and in groups, and provides advice and information on practical problems and opportunities for social contact. There are over 100 branches throughout the country. The headquarters address is Cruse House, 126 Sheen Road, Richmond, Surrey TW9 1UR (telephone: 01-940 4818 or 9047). Publications include the monthly *Cruse Chronicle* for members and a wide range of factsheets and helpful leaflets.

The **National Association for Widows** has branches in many parts of the country. The headquarters address is c/o Stafford District Voluntary Service Centre, Chell Road, Stafford ST16 2QA (telephone: 0785 45465). Its *Handbook for widows* (£1.50 plus postage) gives reassurance on the stages of grief and recovery as well as advice on practical matters. The NAW Widows' Advisory Service includes a series of free information booklets on finance and the home.

Bereavement counselling is given by some branches of **Age Concern**: contact the head office at Bernard Sunley House, 60 Pitcairn Road, Mitcham, Surrey CR4 3LL (telephone: 01-640 5431) to find out whether your local branch of Age Concern offers this help. An Age Concern factsheet on *Arranging a funeral* is available free.

Age Concern, Cruse and the National Association for Widows have combined to publish *Survival guide for widows* (£3.50 plus postage).

The Foundation for the Study of Infant Deaths (15 Belgrave Square, London SW1X 8PS, telephone: 01-235 1721) acts as a centre of information about cot death, for parents and for professionals. As well as raising money for research into the causes and prevention of cot death (also called 'sudden infant death syndrome'), it gives personal support to

bereaved families by letter or telephone, provides information leaflets for parents, and puts parents in touch with
formerly bereaved parents who offer an individual befriend-
ing service. Many have formed themselves into groups to
help each other and the newly bereaved.

The Compassionate Friends is a nationwide organisation
of parents whose child has died, offering friendship and
understanding to other bereaved parents. In addition to
telephone calls, letters and personal visits to the newly
bereaved, regional branches hold regular meetings. The
name of your nearest contact can be obtained from the
headquarters: 6 Denmark Street, Bristol BS1 5DQ (telephone:
0272 292778). There are a number of leaflets for bereaved
parents and those wishing to help them.

The **National Council for Voluntary Organisations** (26
Bedford Square, London WC1B 3HU) keeps information on
national voluntary organisations and may be able to suggest
ones which can offer help in specific circumstances – for
example, to bereaved parents or to widows. Information on
local organisations can also be obtained from a local council
for voluntary service.

Death brings with it many problems for the family, and a
social worker may be able to help at this time by arranging
for practical services that are required – for example, concerning the care of children – and by trying to help the
bereaved work through their often painful and complex
feelings following the death.

PENSIONS AND OTHER STATE BENEFITS

Following the death of a spouse or close relative, you may become eligible for certain payments from the state.

The Department of Health and Social Security administers all national insurance benefits. It issues explanatory leaflets for different categories of people and situations – for example, on widow's benefit and on the death grant – and these are available free at any social security office.

A list of relevant DHSS leaflets is given on page 127.

National insurance benefits are paid to the dependants of those who had paid, or had credited to them, national insurance contributions during their lifetime.

You are not expected to know what contributions have been paid or credited when you apply for any benefits. The DHSS keeps records of everyone's contributions.

The number of contributions required varies according to the type of benefit claimed. When the number of contributions does not fully qualify for certain benefits, a reduced rate may be paid.

If you need to find out about claiming any benefits after someone has died abroad, write to the overseas branch of the Department of Health and Social Security, Newcastle upon Tyne NE9 1YX.

☆ Under the Social Security Act 1986, parts of which are due to come into operation in April 1987 (the rest by April 1988), considerable changes will be introduced regarding the different types of state benefit and the qualifying criteria. The following pages describe the situation up to April 1987.

death grant

The death grant is a nominal sum (maximum £30) normally paid to the executors; otherwise, it is paid to the person meeting the funeral expenses or to the next of kin.

Payment of the grant depends on there being an appropriate national insurance contribution record.

The amount of the grant is determined by the age of the person who died. For a child up to three the grant is £9, for a child between three and five years it is £15, and for anyone between the ages of six and seventeen it is £22.50. From the age of eighteen, the death grant is £30 for a man who was born on or after 5 July 1893 and for a woman who was born on or after 5 July 1898. A reduced grant of £15 is payable for anyone born ten years before those dates. Anyone older than that does not qualify for a death grant.

The death grant can be applied for on the back of the certificate of registration of death (form BD8, given by the registrar for national insurance purposes) or claimed on a form (BD1) which you can get from a social security office. If you have not already sent in the form BD8, evidence of death must accompany your completed application for a death grant. With the application form should also go the deceased's marriage certificate, if married; also any national insurance contribution card and any Department of Health and Social Security payment books not yet handed back.

☆ The death grant is due to be abolished from April 1987. In its place, a person responsible for meeting the funeral expenses will be able to apply for a payment from the new 'social fund' to cover the reasonable cost of a funeral, but only if he or she is in receipt of one of the qualifying benefits – supplementary benefit, family income supplement or housing benefit.

widow's benefit

Widow's benefit is an omnibus term used by the Department of Health and Social Security for a number of payments to which a woman may become entitled following her husband's death. A widow qualifies only if her husband's national insurance contribution record satisfies the appropriate conditions; her own contributions do not count.

Only the lawful widow can claim any widow's benefit on a man's death. If the marriage had been annulled or dissolved by divorce, the woman is not regarded as his lawful widow. If she marries again while under the age of sixty, she loses her widow's benefit from her previous marriage.

A widow does not apply specifically for any one benefit but makes her claim on a detailed form (form BW1), available at any social security office or by applying for it on form BD8. On form BW1 she is asked to give particulars of herself and her late husband and of any children under the age of nineteen. She should send off the form as soon as possible and not later than three months after her husband's death in order not to lose any of the benefits. If she can send her marriage and birth certificates, too, it will speeds things up.

A widow who qualifies for benefit normally gets a book of weekly orders, cashable at a post office. Each order is valid for three months and if it is not cashed within that time, she has to apply for a replacement; if not cashed within 12 months, the benefit for that week is generally lost. A widow eligible for a pension or a widowed mother's allowance can choose to be paid four-weekly or quarterly in arrear instead. She has to fill in a separate application form (in leaflet NI 105) for payment direct into a bank or girobank account or a national savings bank or building society investment account.

Widow's benefit is not affected by any earnings a widow

may have or income from investments. It is, however, subject to income tax and may be affected by other social security benefits payable to her or similar payments out of public funds, such as a war widow's pension or a training allowance.

If her late husband's contributions were insufficient for her to receive the full, or any, widow's benefit, she will be informed in writing. She has a right of appeal to the social security appeal tribunal if she disagrees with the decision. This is explained in the notification, and a citizens advice bureau can be asked about the procedure.

National insurance benefits are reviewed by the government at least once a year. The current amounts for the benefits described in the following pages are on page 125.

widow's allowance

A widow under the age of sixty or whose husband was under sixty-five or had chosen to continue working after the age of sixty-five without drawing his pension, receives an allowance every week for the first 26 weeks after her husband's death, provided his contribution record entitles her to it. Increases for dependent children may also be payable.

☆ From April 1987, instead of the widow's allowance for 26 weeks, a widow will receive a tax-free lump sum payment (proposed amount £1000).

widow's pension

After the first 26 weeks' allowance, a widow without children may receive a weekly pension, depending on her age and on her husband's contribution record.

contribution requirements

The requirements for a widow's pension are that the husband had paid 50 contributions of any class at any time before 6 April 1975 or had paid contributions on earnings of at least 50 times the weekly lower earnings limit for the payment of contributions in any one tax year from 6 April 1975 to 5 April 1978 or had paid contributions on earnings of at least 52 times the weekly lower earnings limit for the payment of contributions in any one tax year from 6 April 1978.

For benefit to be paid at the standard rate, the husband must have paid or been credited with contributions equivalent to the level of contributions paid on earnings of at least the minimum specified level (currently, 52 times the weekly lower earnings limit) in a specified number of tax years during his working life.

The husband's working life is normally taken to be the number of complete tax years in the period from 6 April before his sixteenth birthday to 5 April before his death, or before he reached the age of sixty-five if earlier. If he was already contributing to the insurance scheme before 5 July 1948, however, the period will count from the tax year in which he entered insurance or 6 April 1936, whichever is later. If he was over sixteen on 5 July 1948 and entered insurance on or after that date, the period for the calculation of his working life will begin on 6 April 1948.

The number of years required for a standard rate of basic pension is calculated as follows:

	number of years required
2 to 10 years in working life	the number of years of the working life, minus 1
11 to 20 years in working life	the number of years of the working life, minus 2
21 to 30 years in working life	the number of years of the working life, minus 3
31 to 40 years in working life	the number of years of the working life, minus 4
over 40 years in working life	the number of years of the working life, minus 5

If the number of years in which the specified minimum level

of contribution is reached (known as the qualifying years) is less than the requisite number, a proportionately reduced rate of basic pension will be payable provided the condition about the minimum of 50 (or 52) payments is satisfied and that at least a quarter of the requisite number of qualifying years has been achieved.

additional pension

The pension may include an additional (earnings-related) pension based on the husband's earnings as an employed person from April 1978. The pension will be 1¼ per cent of his earnings between a lower and upper weekly limit set for each year. If he was a member of a contracted-out occupational pension scheme, part of his widow's additional pension will be payable by that scheme.

widow under sixty without dependent children

The pension a widow gets depends on her age at the time of her husband's death.

A widow under the age of forty at that time does not get a widow's pension.

A woman who was forty or over but under fifty when her husband died gets a widow's pension calculated on a sliding scale according to her age. This scale starts at 30 per cent of the standard rate for a woman aged forty at that time and goes in 7 per cent steps, so that a widow aged forty-nine when her husband died gets 93 per cent of the standard rate.

A widow who is fifty or over but under sixty at the time of her husband's death gets the full standard rate of basic pension.

☆ From April 1987, the age at which widow's pension is payable, at the full or a reduced rate, is to be raised by 5 years: a widow under 45 will get no pension.

widow over sixty

If a woman is sixty or over at the time of her husband's death and they had both been drawing the retirement pension, she can ask on form BD8 for her retirement pension to be changed to the rate for a widow. She may also be entitled to extra basic pension if her husband had deferred his retirement after he was sixty-five. In addition, she will receive half any graduated pension he was getting.

If a widow is already drawing a retirement pension based on her own contributions but a pension based on her late husband's contributions would be at a higher rate than her own, her pension can be replaced by one based on his.

A widow can inherit the whole of her late husband's basic and additional pension. If she is entitled to a retirement pension based on her own contributions, she can add the two retirement pensions together. The sum of the basic pensions is limited to the full rate of basic pension, and the additional pensions to the maximum that a single contributor could have earned from April 1978.

A man whose wife dies when they are both over retirement age can draw a pension derived partly from her contribution record and partly from his own, in exactly the same way as a widow can do, up to the same maximum.

A woman who is not yet drawing retirement pension when her husband dies may qualify for a widow's pension, even if she goes on working. Once she has retired, or reaches the age of sixty-five, she inherits half her husband's graduated pension to add to her retirement pension as well as any of her own.

widow with dependent children

A widow gets an additional allowance from the date of her husband's death for each child under school-leaving age, or who is under nineteen and a full-time student or apprentice, or whose schooling or apprenticeship has been interrupted because of illness. A widow can only claim the extra allowance for a child who was or would have been treated as part of her late husband's family, and normally only for a child living with her. This payment is in addition to the child benefit she draws.

A widow with dependent children receives a widowed mother's personal allowance for herself as well as the payment for each child. A widow who is expecting a child by her late husband gets the personal allowance and, after the child is born, the additional amount for the child.

A widow continues to get the widowed mother's personal allowance if any child over sixteen but under nineteen who has left school is still living with her; she does not get an additional allowance for the child. A widow who is under forty at the time when her children cease to qualify her for widowed mother's allowance then gets nothing. A widow who by that time is over forty and under sixty gets the appropriate widow's pension for her age then.

A divorced woman may on the death of her former husband get the allowance for any child in her family whom he had been maintaining. She can apply for this allowance on form CS1, available from any social security office.

war widow's pension
If her husband had been in the armed forces and his death could be attributed to his military service, or he had been drawing war pension constant attendance allowance, the widow should write to the Department of Health and Social Security, Norcross, Blackpool FY5 3TA, explaining the circumstances fully, and asking if she is entitled to a war widow's pension.

supplementary benefit or family income supplement

A widow (or anyone else) who is not in full-time work and whose average weekly income is below a specified minimum can claim a supplementary allowance or pension. An explanatory leaflet (SB1) is available at all post offices and includes a claim form. An officer of the Department of Health and Social Security will call to discuss the position unless the claimant chooses to go to the office to give the required information about his or her financial circumstances.

A widow (or any other lone parent) who is in paid employment for at least 24 hours a week and has at least one child living with her under the age of sixteen, or over sixteen but under nineteen and still at school, may be eligible for family income supplement, if her normal gross weekly income is below a certain level. The level of income below which she qualifies depends on the number and ages of the children. Certain items of income, including child benefit but not widow's benefit, are disregarded from the calculation of the family's weekly income.

The amount of supplement payable is half the difference between the weekly income and the appropriate level, subject to a maximum. A leaflet and claim form (FIS 1) can be obtained from social security offices and post offices.

☆ Under the provisions of the Social Security Act 1986, supplementary benefit will be replaced by 'income support' (a basic allowance plus premiums for particular groups of people, such as lone parents and pensioners) and family income supplement replaced by 'family credit'.

industrial death benefit

If someone dies as the result of an accident at work or of one of the 50-odd prescribed industrial diseases, his dependants can claim industrial death benefit. Most people working for an employer and certain office-holders are covered for industrial death benefit. There are no contribution conditions for the benefit and it does not matter how long the dead person had been employed in that occupation.

In the midst of the widow's claim form BW1, there is a question asking whether she claims that her husband's death was due to an industrial accident or a prescribed industrial disease. If the answer is yes, she should send the full death certificate issued by the registrar because this states the medical cause (or causes) or death.

Even a widow without children gets a weekly pension; if she was over fifty at the time of her husband's death, she gets a pension at a higher rate. A widow who was pregnant when her husband died or who is permanently unable to support herself also gets the higher rate pension.

A widower who is permanently incapable of supporting himself and who was wholly or mainly maintained by his wife receives a weekly pension if she dies as the result of an industrial accident or prescribed industrial disease. This is the only circumstance when a man receives a national insurance pension on the death of his wife. He should claim on form BI 200, available from social security offices, sending the appropriate death certificate and his marriage certificate.

Other dependants, such as parents or other close relatives who had been supported by a man or woman whose death resulted from an industrial accident or prescribed industrial disease, can also claim on form BI 200 for a benefit which will be either a weekly payment or a lump sum. The fact that one person is getting a death benefit in respect of an industrial death does not necessarily preclude another dependant getting one, too.

☆ The provisions of the Social Security Act 1986 will affect the payment of industrial death benefit for a widow.

orphans

A person who takes into his family an orphaned child may be entitled to a guardian's allowance. Although the payment is called a guardian's allowance, it is not necessary to assume legal guardianship to qualify. Usually the allowance is paid only when both parents are dead, but it can sometimes be paid after the death of one parent – for instance, where the other is missing or cannot be traced, or where the parents were divorced and the other is neither maintaining the child nor subject to any liability for maintenance. The allowance is not awarded unless one of the child's parents was a british subject or had been resident in this country for a specified length of time. It is paid only if the guardian qualifies for child benefit for the child.

Application for a guardian's allowance should be made on form BG 1, which can be obtained from any social security office. A claim should be submitted not later than three months after the child joins the family, otherwise the guardian may lose some benefit.

When there is no one to take charge of a child, the local authority social services department should be told and will assume responsibility for the child. If at all possible, children of the same family are kept together.

widows and national insurance contributions

A woman who immediately before her husband died had full liability for national insurance contributions (that is, she was required to pay standard rate class 1 contributions when employed and class 2 contributions when self-employed) continues to do so as a widow.

However, if she was paying reduced-rate class 1 contributions when employed immediately prior to the date her husband died, she continues to have reduced liability until the end of the tax year (5 April) in which her husband died if he died before 1 October or until the end of the following tax year if he died on or after 1 October. Or she can change to full liability straightaway.

There is no liability for a woman to pay any national insurance contributions after she reaches the age of sixty.

Leaflet NI 51 gives full details of the contribution position of widows and how payment of full or reduced contributions may affect entitlement to national insurance benefits. A copy of the leaflet is issued to newly widowed women; any woman in doubt about her pension can ask the staff at her local social security office for further information and advice. If there is a significant gap in her recent contributions record, she may be able to fill this by making voluntary (class 3) contributions now.

A widow who has responsibilities at home, such as bringing up a child under sixteen, can have her future right to a basic pension on her own contributions record protected without the need to pay voluntary contributions. She cannot qualify for this protection, however, for any tax year during which she has retained the right to pay reduced-rate contributions. Leaflet NP 27, *Looking after someone at home*, gives further details.

NATIONAL INSURANCE BENEFITS: AMOUNTS

Until April 1987, the weekly amounts payable for the benefits described in the preceding pages are:

widow's benefit

widow's allowance for first 26 weeks	£54.20
widow's basic pension	£38.70
widowed mother's personal allowance	£38.70
widow's or guardian's or divorced mother's allowance per child	£8.05

industrial death pension:	
widow over fifty	£39.25
widow under fifty	£11.61
widower	£39.25

family income supplement

The *weekly income limits* are:
for one child £98.60 if under age 11
            £99.60 if aged 11 to 15
            £100.60 if aged 16 or over
plus for each additional child:
            £11.65 if under age 11
            £12.65 if aged 11 to 15
            £13.65 if aged 16 or over
The *maximum payment per week* is:
aged under 11   one child £25.30, plus £2.55 for each additional child
aged 11 to 15   one child £25.80, plus £3.05 for each additional child
aged 16 or over one child £26.30, plus £3.55 for each additional child

supplementary benefit

The *scale rates* are:	*ordinary rate*	*long-term and pensioner rate*
single householder	£29.80	£37.90
non-householder	£23.85	£30.35
plus for each dependent child:		
aged under 11	£10.20	£10.20
aged 11 to 15	£15.30	£15.30
aged 16 to 17	£18.40	£18.40
aged over 18	£23.85	£23.85

APPLICATION FORMS FOR GRANTS, ALLOWANCES AND PENSIONS

BD8	from registrar, on back of certificate of registration/notification of death	to apply for form BD1 and for form BW1, or for an adjustment in retirement pension for a widow
BD1	from a DHSS office, or or by sending form BD8	to apply for a death grant
BW1	from a DHSS office, or by sending form BD8	to claim widow's benefits
NI105	from a DHSS office	to apply for payment of benefit direct into banks or building societies
BI200	from a DHSS office	for widower and other dependants to apply for industrial death benefits
CS1	from a DHSS office	for a divorced woman to claim allowance for child(ren) on death of former husband
BG1	from a DHSS office	to apply for guardian's allowance for the support of an orphan
FIS1	from a DHSS office and post offices	to apply for family income supplement
SB1	from a DHSS office and post offices	to apply for supplementary pension or allowance

LEAFLETS ISSUED BY THE DHSS

D 49	What to do after a death

about payments and qualifications:

NI 49	Death grant
NP 35	Your benefit as a widow for the first 26 weeks
NP 36	Your benefit as a widow after the first 26 weeks
NI 10	Industrial death benefits for widows and other dependants
NI 93	Child's special allowance
NI 14	Guardian's allowance
NI 196	Social security benefit rates and earnings rules
NI 105	Payment direct into banks or building societies: retirement pensions and widow's benefits
NP 32	Your retirement pension
NP 32A	Your retirement pension if you are widowed or divorced
FB 2	Which benefit?
FB 3	Help for one-parent families
CH 11	One-parent benefit for people bringing up children alone
MPL 152	War widows: war pensions, allowances and welfare services
MPL 154	Rates of war pensions and allowances
SB 16	Lump sum payments for people on supplementary benefit

about paying national insurance contributions:

NI 51	Widows: guidance about NI contributions and benefits
NI 208	National insurance contribution rates and SSP rates
NI 40	National insurance contributions for employees
NI 41	National insurance guide for the self-employed
NI 42	National insurance voluntary contributions
NI 27A	National insurance contributions: people with small earnings from self-employment
NI 255	National insurance contributions: direct debit
NP 28	More than one job? your class 1 NI contributions
NP 27	Looking after someone at home: how to protect your pension

These leaflets are available free from any DHSS office.

INLAND REVENUE LEAFLETS

Leaflet IR 45 about what happens when someone dies and leaflet IR 23 about income tax and widows are available free from tax offices.

BEFORE YOUR OWN DEATH

A printed form *Instructions for my next of kin and executors upon my death* is available for 25p from **Age Concern**, Bernard Sunley House, 60 Pitcairn Road, Mitcham, Surrey CR4 3LL. On this, you can put down details of yourself that may be useful when your death is being registered (such as your place of birth, NHS number, details of parents and spouse/s), and information about your possessions, insurance policies, employer, with spaces for the names and addresses of relevant people such as solicitor, bank manager, accountant, tax inspector. You can say on it where you keep important documents – not only your will, but birth certificate, marriage certificate, deeds of house, certificates, savings account books. Your wishes regarding your funeral can also be recorded on the form.

Make sure that your family or whoever you live with, or your executors, know about the form and where it is kept.

The Age Concern form is not intended to take the place of a will and says 'you are strongly advised to make a will even if you do not own very much'.

The property of a person who dies intestate (that is, without leaving a valid will) is divided among his family according to the intestacy rules; if he has no close relatives, it may all go to the Crown.

The Consumer Publication *Wills and probate* explains how to make a will, what to say in it, how to have it witnessed, and what happens if there is no will.

It is quite customary to put into a will whether you wish your body to be cremated or buried, but it is important to let your family know because there may be delay before the will is read.

donating your body

The number of organ transplants being carried out in this country has increased encouragingly, but there is a continual need for more and the waiting lists for transplant and grafting operations are still too long.

Anyone who would like any part of his or her body to be used to save or prolong someone's life should complete one of the small red donor cards available at GPs' surgeries, hospitals, clinics, dispensing chemists, social security offices. The card should be carried with you at all times. It is also sensible to tell your GP and your nearest kin that you have signed a donor card as evidence of your willingness to let parts of your body be used for the treatment of others. If you go into hospital as an inpatient, be sure to tell the ward sister or other senior member of staff that you are a potential donor.

eyes

If you specifically want the cornea of your eyes to be used, you can get in touch with the Royal National Institute for the Blind's prevention of blindness services coordinator (224 Great Portland Street, London W1N 6AA). You will be sent a multi-organ donor card to sign and keep, a leaflet giving information on what is involved, and a letter with details of the appropriate hospital to be contacted in your area.

heart

For heart transplants, the British Heart Foundation issues donor cards on which to express a wish for your heart to be used "for transplantation or, if found unsuitable, for research". The card has to be signed by a next of kin to record that there is no objection to your request. You can remain anonymous. The heart donor card can be obtained from the headquarters of the British Heart Foundation (102 Gloucester Place, London W1H 4DH) or from a regional BHF office (addresses in local telephone directories).

the body
Before expressing a formal wish that your whole body be used for anatomical examination and medical education, you should discuss the matter with your family and next of kin, and tell your executors, because they will have to act quickly after you have died.

To make the arrangements, you should contact the professor of anatomy at your nearest medical school or HM Inspector of Anatomy at the DHSS, Eileen House, 80–94 Newington Causeway, London SE1 6EF. In Scotland, the Scottish Home and Health Department, St Andrew's House, Edinburgh EH1 3DE, can provide information.

requesting cremation

People who wish to be cremated can register with the Cremation Society (Woodcut House, Ashford Road, Hollingbourne, Maidstone, Kent ME17 1XH) under a scheme which the Society calls F.A.T.E. ('Funeral arrangements for use by trustees and executors'). The registration fee is £10. The particulars you give about yourself (doctor, next of kin, executor, solicitor, life insurance policies, whereabouts of your will, type of funeral service you would like, any medical donor bequests) are recorded and a copy sent to you, with an identity card for you to carry which asks that the Cremation Society be informed before any funeral arrangements are made on your death.

A note to executors or family on a piece of plain paper is just as valid, albeit less formal. But even if you leave specific instructions that you want – or do not want – your body to be cremated, there is no legal obligation on executors or next of kin to carry out your wishes.

pre-payment for the funeral

If you want to make the arrangements personally for your own funeral, you can approach an undertaker at any time and discuss with him what you want to happen when you die. You can pay in advance towards the expenses but if costs rise in the meantime, the undertaker will claim from your estate any additional amount for increased costs.

The National Association of Funeral Directors has set up a formal scheme for pre-payment of funeral expenses through its members. A leaflet explaining their funeral expenses plan is available from any undertaker who is a member of the NAFD.

You decide initially what payment would be sufficient for the funeral you would like to have (the funeral director will discuss current costs with you). You can choose to pay for this either by a lump sum (minimum £600) there and then or by monthly contributions for a maximum of 20 years – or until your death, if sooner. The sum you have paid for will be increased each year in line with the retail price index (up to a maximum of 10% per annum). When you die, the funeral can be arranged through any NAFD member, and the money built up in the scheme (which is tax-free) will be used to pay for the cost of your funeral.

Similar schemes for anticipating funeral expenses are offered by a few specialist companies on the basis of monthly premium payments or a lump sum (the payment may have to be by lump sum if you are over 65).

Before tying up money in this way towards funeral expenses, consider whether an alternative investment would not be a better buy.

INDEX

some other Consumer Publications

Wills and probate

is a layman's guide to making your will without employing a solicitor and how to administer the estate of someone who has died. For making a will, it tells you how to assess your likely estate, what to consider when appointing executors and a guardian for children. It shows you how to ensure that your will is free from ambiguity: what to say and how to say it, so that your wishes can be carried out without complication, how a will should be signed and witnessed and what to do when you wish to alter your will. It explains the implications of inheritance tax and capital gains tax and points out where and how tax can be saved.

For someone called upon to act as an executor, the probate section of the book is a step-by-step guide through the procedure, including sections on calculating the assets, how to get and fill in the probate forms, carrying out valuations, dealing with the bank and what to do while the accounts of the deceased are frozen, paying inheritance tax and dealing with income tax and capital gains tax, and all the other tasks that need to be performed in order to get a grant of probate. After probate has been granted, the executor has to deal with transferring property, selling or transferring shares, encashing national savings, gathering in the assets and distributing the legacies and bequests to beneficiaries.

The book also explains what happens, and what has to be done, if there is no will and the next of kin have to cope with the administration.

Renting and letting

is a book which helps to clarify the legal position of all who pay rent to occupy their home, and anyone who wants to let property. The law of landlord and tenant is complex and confers rights as well as responsibilities on both sides. The security of a tenant's home, both in the private and the public sector, is safeguarded by law, but a prudent landlord need not be discouraged from letting, provided he fully understands the legal implications. The book explains when a landlord cannot get vacant possession from a tenant, and in what circumstances he can. It includes sections on rent control and getting a fair rent registered, explains the meaning of protected and statutory tenancy and what happens on the death of the original tenant. It deals with the repair obligation of landlords and the various protections a tenant has, including protection from harrassment and eviction and explains the council tenant's rights, including the right to buy the rented property.

Which? way to buy, sell and move house

takes you through all the stages of moving to another home – considering the pros and cons of different places, house hunting, viewing, having a survey, making an offer, getting a mortgage, completing the purchase, selling the present home. It explains the legal procedures and the likely costs. Buying and selling at an auction and in Scotland are specifically dealt with. The practical arrangements for the move and for any repairs or improvements to the new house are described. Advice is given for easing the tasks of sorting, packing and moving possessions, people and pets, with a removal firm or by doing it yourself, and for making the day of the move go smoothly.

The legal side of buying a house

for buying an owner-occupied house in England or Wales, this book will guide you step by step through the legal procedure. It explains what is involved and follows in detail the whole process of doing your own conveyancing – from placing a deposit, obtaining all the relevant forms and filling them in, dealing with the Land Registry and local authority, to exchange of contracts and, finally, completion. Even if you have decided that doing your own conveyancing would be too time-consuming or difficult for you, this book will help you check what your solicitor is doing at each stage. The book also deals with the legally less complicated procedure of selling your house.

Approaching retirement

will help you prepare for a happy and rewarding retirement. It tells you when to start planning for it (probably earlier than you think), how to adapt to having more free time, what benefits and concessions you will get, and how to cope financially. There is information about pensions, from the state or an employer, and tax, about how to find work in retirement, about organising your finances to provide an income and minimise your tax bill. The book also advises on the decision whether to move or stay put, on keeping well, and on adjusting to a different daily routine.

What will my pension be?

examines in detail the different pension arrangements currently in existence – from the state, an employer's scheme, if self-employed – detailing what benefits they may provide, what restrictions apply, how much it will cost you now and how much you can expect to receive on retirement, how tax affects the payments.

Earning money at home

explains how to brush up a skill or hobby into a money-making venture. It gives advice on organising your family and domestic life, on advertising your activities, costing and selling your work, dealing with customers. There is information on statutory and financial requirements for insurance, tax, accounts, VAT, employing others. The book suggests ways in which your experience from a previous job could be utilised, or a skill or hobby developed to a professional standard, or how unexploited energy and ability can be used profitably. Suggestions are made for improving your skills to a higher standard, and the names and addresses are given of organisations that might be helpful.

Starting your own business

for people who have the courage, imagination and stamina to try a new venture on their own, this is a competent guide to help them through the essential steps. It advises on defining precisely what product or skill you have to offer, how to raise the necessary capital and cope with legal requirements. It deals with all the financial aspects: pricing the product, calculating overheads and cash flow, keeping accounts and other records, dealing with taxes including VAT, marketing and selling, premises and insurance. Throughout, sources of advice and information are given to help the small businessman make a success of going it alone.

Living with stress

helps the reader to cope with the many and various stresses in life, including the stress of loneliness, sickness, bereavement. It points to the more common warning signs and indicates what can be done to adapt where nothing can be changed.

Understanding cancer

explains the nature and causes of the disease most people
find more frightening than any other. It tells you how to
recognise some of the symptoms and avoid some of the
risks, and explains how cancer is diagnosed. It goes into the
details of various forms of treatment: surgery, radiotherapy,
chemotherapy, including their possible side effects, and
takes an objective look at the role of alternative/complemen-
tary therapies. It describes some of the advances in cancer
research but does not pretend that these will soon provide
the long awaited cure. The book deals with advanced cancer
and terminal care but stresses that cancer must not be
regarded as inevitably fatal.

Children, parents and the law

describes the legal responsibilities and rights of a parent,
and of a child towards parents, so far as they exist. It deals
with illegitimacy, when things go wrong in the family, with
education, if a child comes up against the law, when a child
has to go into the care of the local authority, and explains
what is involved in custodianship, guardianship, adoption,
fostering. It sets out at what ages a child can carry out
specific activities – from buying a pet to getting married.
There is a section explaining the effects of a child being
injured and of the death of one or both parents.

Consumer Publications are available from Consumers'
Association, Castlemead, Gascoyne Way, Hertford
SG14 1LH, and from booksellers.